FACE TO FACE WITH PANIC ATTACKS

how to overcome panic attacks and feel good.

BY ROMOLO PERSICHETTI

PREFACE

The book tells the point of view of one of the many people visited by Mr. Panic, who generally presents with an attack. I don't know how else to say it. The phenomenon we are dealing with is therefore that of the so-called "Panic attacks". The use of capital letters is not a spelling error but a conscious choice. I would like to point out straight away that I am not a therapist, but simply a person who will talk about his experience on the subject. I will talk about how the first episode happened and the others afterwards, as well as the various forms in which it manifests itself. In the manuscript I will also include the testimonies of other people I have met who like me have gone through this...let's call it an inconvenience for now. The phenomenon of panic attacks affects millions of people around the world and I know they will be the ones reading me. For everyone else I advise against reading. It seems that by naming it and knowing it, sooner or later it will reveal itself to those who, even through hearsay, become aware of it. This happened to me so I draw this conclusion. Maybe Mr. Panic would never have come to see me if I hadn't heard about him, or maybe he would? Who can say? In books, in stories, there is usually a protagonist and one or more antagonists. Undoubtedly the protagonist is Panic, this entity that strikes the strong (another deduction of mine) and the antagonists are those who have known him. Having said that, let's move on to the facts.

Chapter 1
"How I consider Panic and how I met him"

Panic is a friend to me. Yes, you understood correctly. In hindsight I can say that I even considered him an ally. He taught me many things as I will say. The reason why I'm writing about it may seem bizarre, but after two years from the last episode, and from the awareness of having made peace with us and having closed the accounts, a day ago he returned. A quick visit, but with a great impact. As usual he arrived without warning, he knocked loudly, he stayed in my mind for about twenty minutes and left. His visit left me stunned. What does he want? It was in the evening after an overall calm day, in the previous weeks I had received a few visits from his cousins, Anxiety and Stress. But I didn't worry too much. I knew well that usually before a visit his cousins stop by to say hello; but after two years I didn't think at all that he might show up again. So I sat down in my chair and started asking myself questions. I came to the conclusion that having had a good and successful relationship with him, it was my clear duty to share my story to make him known in a new light. I don't know how to explain it, it's like I feel indebted to him. Generally, panic attacks have a negative meaning, so much so that you even go to the doctor and even take drugs (which I have never done and which I advise against). I wonder and I ask you, what if they were called 'Panic's caresses'? Or the "Panic visits?" would change a lot. Do you agree? Yes I know, maybe you're wondering if I've really ever had panic attacks and if I know what it feels like. Like me, you know that often in those moments only one thought revolves in various forms in the head: "imminent death" without any ifs or buts, when he takes possession of our mind, imminent death is the only thing you can think of. to think, the only frequency on which to stay tuned for 20 to 60 minutes. Radio Panico transmits only in low frequencies. I'll just tell you that the first time, in 2017, I was driving on the highway at night, to travel five hours to go to my grandmother's funeral. So I wasn't exactly enthusiastic about that trip, after about an hour, while I was overtaking a lorry with a trailer, I started to get short of breath, I felt pain in my chest and arm and I was shaking my legs, my sister's future husband was in the car with me. I don't know how, I managed to get back on the road without having an accident and I pulled over. Obviously it wasn't a three-lane motorway with a nice wide emergency lane, no, it was two lanes and the emergency one was a narrow one. My sister's partner, scared, asks me what's happening, but I didn't know what to answer. I didn't know what the hell had gotten into me, I thought I was having an imminent heart attack. But then, a light bulb went on. It was the panic attack that I had heard about from a friend of mine who had met him before me and so I say, it's a panic attack. Yes, that's fine... it seems easy when put that way. For our first meeting he decided to spend the entire journey with me, which lasted 9 hours. Obviously after about a quarter of an hour I managed to get my sister's partner to drive but even if I didn't look at the odometer, every time it exceeded 80 km/h I got nervous, I even saw the road distorted, something I'd never seen before. The subsequent ones, as I will tell later, were not less powerful and devastating, also because they always happened while driving like the first time, I will talk about this later, because the way in which it occurs the first time according to my experience and that of others , is very important, because it occurs as a sort of "stimulation induced" by the first episode. I made this incipit because perhaps from how I started it might seem to you that I hadn't taken the topic seriously or that I wanted to joke about it. None of this, I'm serious when I say that he was a good friend and in the analysis and lessons I learned from him you will find the reason for this statement. I would add, however, that joking a little about what scares us helps to reduce the problem. Let's say, as I anticipated, that the name, the definition, qualifies it very badly. Attack! An attack.. synonymous with violent aggression.. that's why, to resize it and make you change your perspective, I want you, like me, to imagine him as a person. He is abstract, in some ways he is an illusion. Well, I could even say that he is the best illusionist I have ever met. No one like him is able to control your mind even for a short time and make you feel absolutely real emotions and physical sensations. A sort of "meta-verse" which he enters without the aid of technology. Which let me tell you is amazing and awesome in itself. Fantastic comes from fantasy... so keep this concept with you too. I will talk later about the techniques I have tested for when you experience the phenomenon. Quick and easy techniques to deal with him, he is the protagonist when he enters our lives, and we are the antagonists who must prevent him from entering. It's like a game, he thinks he's a sentry guarding a space... how do you imagine this space? Is it round? Is it square? Are there fences? Imagine, think of your own dimension. If your body and mind were a shape, what shape would they have? I will insist a lot on imagination because it is a fundamental step. The human brain thinks mainly, not exclusively, in images. With a little training that you will do by reading the following you will be able to keep it at bay, and when you are strong enough you will see that Panic will no longer come to disturb you. And if he also visits after a long absence, think of it as a visit from a friend you haven't seen in a long time. Knowing how to communicate with him, knowing how to duel with him and knowing that he is basically a joker will put you in a dominant position compared to him. If you experience the problem personally, you know that in this phase of your life he dominates you and you suffer. He is big, he is strong and you are the prey. I want to get you to reverse this ratio of 10 to 1 and bring you to a ratio of 1 to 10. This result is achieved by slowly reducing the ratio until it reverses it. Maybe it seems impossible to you now, maybe you've been in therapy for months, maybe you take some tranquilizers, maybe your circle of acquaintances is aware of this problem of yours and so maybe you've gotten used to the idea of living with it. Well this is exactly the wrong attitude. I went through this phase too. The surrender phase. At a certain point after yet another episode I told a friend of mine that I would never go back to the way I was before. I was convinced and resigned. Convinced and resigned to the idea of no longer driving a car. Something that I have always loved... and which at a certain point started to scare me to the point that I didn't dare go further than 10 kilometers from my house and in the first few months even going a short distance was a drama. But then something happens, if your nature is that of a warrior, if you don't have this nature, however, you can still decide to let it go. He goes away when you give him what he wants. And what does panic want from your life? I tell you. I know this. He wants you to get out of the cage you've locked yourself in! He wants you out of prison! It's you your jailer! That's why I called him a friend, an ally. He was scary, he had a brusque manner, not at all nice, sometimes I even risked losing my life because of him. Then I'll tell you. But he was there to help me but I was like a wild animal caught in a net that sees a man approaching, do you know that? Have you ever seen any videos or documentaries? Imagine you are a wild animal. Well, now imagine that you got caught in a trap or net or fell into a hole. Can you see the details? Well. What usually happens when humans find themselves having to free one of these animals? That as soon as they see the man they begin to struggle like never before, they are pervaded by terror and sometimes the more agitated they become in an attempt to escape and free themselves, the more they become entangled. The most aggressive animals even attack, if they can bite they bite, if they have claws they scratch. Go and explain to them that what they are running from is actually what will save them. In the case of particularly dangerous animals such as bears, lions or tigers it is even necessary to sedate them before approaching them. This is why some forms of panic lead the subject to freeze completely, in some cases even falling to the ground. Well. At this point, if you stopped reading the book you would certainly understand one thing. My thoughts, my considerations on this topic are totally different from everything that is said about panic attacks, such as that "they are disorders" "pathologies" etc. I tell you that Mr. Panic's interventions in your life are not the problem, but the solution. So if he happens to you again now you know, that at least after he has left your mind, you have to start asking yourself questions.

Ask yourself the questions and give yourself the answers. You are unhappy, you are stuck in a situation, you have received visits from cousins of Panic, Anxiety and Stress and you have chased them away, you have ignored them, you have tried to send them away in every way and you thought you had solved it with a tranquilizer, a psychologist or maybe a holiday for a few days, right? He never comes without those other two visiting you first. Generally when you ignore or repress Anxiety and/or Stress they get angry, go to their cousin and say: "- Hey Panic, there's someone who really doesn't listen to us. He doesn't listen to us, he doesn't question himself, he doesn't stop even ten minutes a day to understand what the fuck is happening to him. You, who are bigger and stronger than us, can you intervene?" - And he, like a good cousin, takes charge for the honor of the family, give me the term. And so one day you get this life shock, a bucket of freezing water while you're in your underwear and it's cold outside. And what happens there? What is your reaction? How did you react after giving him a name? And again, how long did it take you to name it? To admit that you had, not a problem, but the problem? Let's see if I guess right. After the second, third maybe certainly with the fourth episode? To be honest, it took me several months, I'm particularly stubborn, and at that stage also foolish and presumptuous. Luckily for me today I can tell you about it and give advice to those who want to accept it, of course.

I defined the triptych "panic, anxiety and stress" as family and the basic concept that I intend to reinforce in your mind is that these three subjects who receive insults and attacks from all people are actually beneficial entities, let me know the term. When you have a problem my darling, it's your problem. Here we are? Except that the elect (remind me of the term, please) must be saved. And therefore from the direction, when a subject is worthy of evolving, they send the support of the three musketeers. Stress and Anxiety, despite having different levels of intensity together, are not enough to cause the level of discomfort of Panic. In fact, on the market you can find many pharmacological products for anxiety disorders, as they call it, or stress but there is no product against panic attacks, simply because it is unstoppable and arrives without warning... at most you can feel it a few seconds before but when you realize it's already too late. Anxiety and stress, on the other hand, when they arrive in your life, accompany you throughout almost the entire day, they stay there, so they are easy to silence. You close them behind a door momentarily so as not to hear them but then you find them there waiting for you, is it true or not? Panic is different, it comes, shakes and hits you and then goes away without saying goodbye and without telling you when it will return. One of the people who wanted to share his experience with me and who we will call Carlo giving a fictitious name, unlike the other cases I will talk about later, and my case, was being treated by a therapist and was constantly taking very powerful anxiolytics and sedatives. He was convinced that this was how he would handle the situation. He felt Ansia's presence and took her drops. Anxiety was fine for a while, then it returned perhaps stronger, and then he switched from drops to pills, unfortunately... but when Panic set in even under the effect of these drugs there was nothing to be done, Carlo called the ambulance saying that he was sick and that they had to come get him as soon as possible. The nice thing is that sometimes based on the operator on duty the ambulance would leave, but most of the time the telephone operator would ask if he was taking any medications or had any allergies and he would respond by mentioning the medications he had taken. And do you know what the operator replied in most cases? Ah ok then increase the dose and wait for it to take effect. Mind you, this is not a criticism of the 118 operators, on the contrary, they were good most of the time at understanding that it was panic and that's it, that's it, so to speak. However, I mention Carlo's experience to underline that there are no drugs against these episodes unless one has a crystal ball or a time machine and knows what time he will receive a visit from Panic... but I think that even in that case It's hard to keep it from crossing our minds. I myself, who have never taken anxiolytics or sedatives despite having experienced Panic in two episodes, ended up calling the ambulance once and going to the emergency room another time a year later. I want to tell you about it for the first time. Now I can almost laugh about it, but always with respect it is understood. At the time I worked as a transporter, I drove for work, I loved driving so much, but for months I had had Anxiety and Stress in the passenger seat due to a whole series of factors, and I had already received Panic in the cabin several times. And if you allow me, of all the situations in which he can visit us, being driving is never the best, in fact it is one of the most dangerous things that can happen to you. I always managed to manage it in the sense that I maintained control until I stopped the vehicle and let the storm pass and then set off again. That time I hadn't had any visits from any of the three for months. I was calm. In some ways I had lowered my guard in my supreme presumption at the time. I was almost at the end of the shift, I had to make the last delivery. I was even happy because I finished early. So nothing could make me think of a visit from my old friend Panico. After unloading the goods, I turn to go back into the cockpit and a black wasp appears out of nowhere and stings me. Let me start by saying that I had already been stung by bees and wasps and thank God I'm not allergic, burning, discomfort yes... swelling around the sting but everything was normal, nothing sensational. Well. I got back on the vehicle and calmly headed back, after less than ten minutes I started scratching myself with a certain intensity, the area around the sting was swollen and very hot, it must have left the stinger inside I thought, and I repeated to myself that it wasn't the first time, thank God the day was over so I could go home and put some ice on. Then suddenly I feel a burning sensation on my face, I look at myself in the rear-view mirror but I wasn't red, I only felt the strong sensation of heat, after a moment the tachycardia and the difficulty in breathing, I parked the van on the side of a secondary road and a second later Panic was in my mind but I didn't recognize it. I had been managing him for over two years and hadn't heard from him in months. I then start to think, or rather delude myself that I was the one thinking, that perhaps I was going into anaphylactic shock, I had some water in the bottle and I threw it on myself in an attempt not to faint. Obviously the road was deserted, not even a dog passed by. So I take my cell phone and call 118.

-" hello good morning, a black bee stung me, I'm not allergic but maybe I'm going into anaphylactic shock please come and get me I can't breathe, help me!!-"

The operator on the phone, very calm and professional, asked me if my tongue was swollen and I replied no.

-"ok then luckily we can rule out shock sir, where are you..etc I'll send the ambulance anyway"-

I call the company and say that I feel ill and that I called the ambulance, I try to stay calm but my legs and arms were shaking I couldn't speak well, maybe that feeling of not being able to do it happens to you too because it's like you're short of air so you know what I'm talking about. After about a quarter of an hour they arrive. I tell the story of what happened but in the meantime I start to feel better despite being weak, I get into the ambulance, they put the IV in me and take blood samples, lying on that stretcher in the cockpit I start to realize that it was my old friend Panico who had given me one of his pranks. But I couldn't stop the ambulance and have them take me back, plus what would they think of me at the company? Obviously I hadn't said anything to anyone... partly out of shame I felt when faced with those events and partly out of pride. The fact is that obviously the blood tests were perfect as usual and nothing significant had emerged. I had to be picked up at the hospital by my brother. He was worried when I told him where he had to come but then I explained to him that it was "just" a panic attack. This went on for another year until I resigned, but I will talk about it later when I talk about the second time I went to the emergency room for the last time, again during work which was one of the causes triggering the malaise from which Anxiety and Stress first, and then Panic definitively managed to save me. Do you recognize yourself in the episode I told? Has it happened to you in a similar way too? I addressed some issues that we will now explore together. Lowering your guard, overestimating yourself by thinking you can handle it yourself and postponing self-analysis, failing to have a problem. So let's open these chapters in the next pages.

Chapter 2

"Lower your guard"

Lowering your guard is inadvisable if after the first few close episodes, as happens for everyone at the beginning, Panic seems to have disappeared. He needs at least a year of work on himself, plus another year to erase the memory from our mind. As if to say, once he visits you he won't leave until he is sure he has saved you, he comes back when you least expect it. The tendency after the first few

times is to carry on as if nothing had happened.
There are basically two types of manifestation:
following a traumatic event which then leaves its
mark for a variable period of time based on the
level of trauma suffered or following the
accumulation in the unconscious of dissatisfaction,
fears and highly stressed situations repressed in the
name of "well yes it's just a bad period it will
pass.." without investigating with self-analysis the
sources that led you to the encounter with Panico.
In this regard, I briefly report the experiences and
testimonies of Elisa and Diego which represent
exactly the two types of access to encounters with
our phenomenon.

Elisa is a woman of about forty years old, with her
father and her sister she runs a jewelery shop in the
city centre. She is a very attractive, intelligent
woman who has been practicing Judo since she was
a child. Her father left her and her sister a
flourishing business in the trade of precious stones,
but thanks to her talent Elisa, who has a strong
artistic vocation which flourished and cultivated
during her years at art high school, when she joined
the company she decided that in addition to selling
jewels of the big names in the sector want to create
their own line to stand out from the competition.
This request of hers is immediately welcomed with
enthusiasm by the whole family, her sister and
partner Giada takes care of the accounts and

negotiations. Together with their father's experience, the girls expand their client base and increase their business, some on the creative side, some on the accounting side. We are in the second decade of the second millennium, it is 2013, the armed robberies that were in vogue between the seventies and the end of the nineties almost no longer happen either in banks or in jewelery shops. Technology, the use of video surveillance and private surveillance, combined with armored doors with separate opening, now discourage the vast majority of criminals. Yet one afternoon in October, on a Tuesday, Elisa's life suddenly changes. It's around 6pm, her sister Giada goes out to go to Pilates class like every Tuesday and the old father who is close to retirement, considering the working day and the total absence of customers decides to return home. Elisa follows him with her gaze as he approaches his car from the shop window, she seems to greet someone, then she glimpses an elderly couple arm in arm, well dressed, exchanging a few words with the old man who gets back into the car and leaves. The two gentlemen approach the window and look at the jewels on display, Elisa observes them from the counter and when she meets the lady's gaze the two smile at each other. Then the woman nods to her husband in the direction of the front door. So the two approach and ring the bell of the double

armored door that allows access to the shop. Elisa
is calm and blissful, what her mind sees are only an
elderly couple who had greeted her father shortly
before her, she does not feel the slightest danger.
So he presses the opening button and the two enter.
There will be a maximum of three meters from the
entrance door to the counter. Elisa doesn't notice
anything and welcomes them with a formal
greeting: -"Good evening gentlemen"-
-" Good evening to you Elisa "- replies the lady,
who despite the wrinkles on her face has a very
youthful voice. But for our jeweler it is not a
relevant detail. The man on the other hand doesn't
speak, he just smiles. The two are still arm in arm.
-"Your father told us his name, we are old
customers and we saw a pendant in the window
that we would like to evaluate as a gift for our
granddaughter who is graduating" - Said the lady
So Elisa opens the gate on the counter and goes
towards the window to understand which of the
jewels they were interested in. The woman leaves
her husband's arm and moves towards the shop
window, Elisa almost joins her, her eyes are on the
woman's hand which indicates a point on the
display. In this dynamic Elisa has her back to the
man. It is precisely by looking at that hand with
smooth skin that Elisa detects an anomaly, she
looks at the woman's face, she realizes that she is
wearing a mask, the kind used by some actors, but

it is already too late. Her man behind her grabs her forearm and twists it backwards and brings her to him, placing his other hand over her mouth and pulling her head back. The two are now stuck together, the man's mouth is close to Elisa's ear and he shouts at her: -"Stop and shut up, whore! He stops and changes and tightens his grip on her mouth. The woman meanwhile she takes a small pistol out of her purse and points it under the nose of the unfortunate woman, saying: -"now my husband will let you go and you will give us all the jewels in the shop window as if you were renewing the display, you must be quick and keep in mind that you'll have to have your back to the window, one nod from you to a passerby, one shout and I'll shoot the whole magazine at you, do you understand whore?"-
Elisa was paralyzed by fear of her, even though she was an expert judo practitioner with a firearm pointed at her and a strong man who physically immobilized her she couldn't move.
-"Let's see if the whore has understood that she must stay quiet and still"- says the man
-"let's see" - the woman replies
So he took his hand away from Elisa's mouth and moved it like a mannequin behind a screen that shielded them from the shop window, and with his free hand he opened the zip on the back of her dress and then slipped his hand inside her bra and

began to touch her breasts. Elisa was paralyzed by her fear, her heart was beating in her throat but she was unable to move or say a word while he continued to grope her with vigor and insistence.
-"it seems to me that the whore has understood" - said the woman with an evil grin. So the man took his hand out of her dress, grabbed her hair and whispered in her ear to go behind the screen, stand with her back to the window and pass him all the boxes quickly. However, Elisa was still blocked so the woman approached her again, pointing the weapon back in her face and saying: "Do you want me to start it again?" -
at that moment Elisa regained part of her motor skills, she went to the shop window with trembling legs and in a minute passed everything on display, then she was taken by the arm again and taken behind the counter from where she was forced by the man to reopen the door held open by the woman. The two disappeared, all, our protagonist tells me, in less than five minutes, the longest five minutes of her entire life, time seemed to never pass. She wasn't able to immediately raise the alarm, she put herself on the ground behind the counter, she started to run out of breath, she couldn't breathe, she couldn't get up, she started to think that she was going to die there. After about half an hour in the grip of our friend Panico, she called the police, on the phone she barely managed

to say: "I've been robbed, come help me". Now you may be wondering how I can call panic a 'friend' in this story. Then try to think about what could have happened if our friend Panico hadn't blocked Elisa. Beyond his methods, the difficulty in breathing, the physical block, the terror of dying there alone, etc.. beyond this, let's hypothesize, absurdly, that Panico had not intervened on Elisa during those excited minutes, and let's say that Elisa had tried to free herself from the man's grip, perhaps while he had a hand between her breasts. With a gun pointed at you and facing two professionals, not two desperate people, what could have happened? The patch would have been worse than the hole, a gunshot to the leg or worse, in a vital point, not worth all the gold in the world. If instead of two professionals there had been two desperate people, the risk of getting hit increased exponentially. Can you now have a different perspective? Do you agree that Panico saved Elisa's life? Yes I would say yes. Obviously then, Panic which in this case arrives following a trauma with a decidedly strong emotional impact, exacts a toll... the price to pay is his company for a variable amount of time as I said before. But better five years with Panic than much worse consequences, right? Well. After a similar experience, Elisa told me that she had to follow a therapeutic path for post traumatic stress syndrome and the resulting panic attacks. Her therapy

obviously included abstention from work for over
three months, the medically supervised use of drugs
to help her sleep in the following days immediately
after the events and real cognitive rehabilitation for
the following months. Even while staying at home
either alone or in her company, Elisa says that
every slightest noise in the house or outside caused
her agitation and strong worry. The closeness of
her husband, children and family was fundamental
in speeding up her recovery time. However, she
tells me, after the first three months at home the
following months were no less difficult. She too
had to stop and pull over on her way home to work
because she was suffering from panic. The mind
after a similar trauma overwrites reality and the tare
on the basis of an experience lived as if it were
current even when it is not. The power of our mind
is literally scary. That's why I tell you that not
letting your guard down is essential. Because once
an apparent normality has been re-established,
everything must be rewritten all mental programs
that have been modified following the triggering
event. The human mind creates associations, which
in basic form are either positive, negative or
neutral. Let's take a practical example on Elisa's
case. Previously, going to work was an activity
considered neutral by her mind. After the traumatic
episode, the exact same action, going to work, was
considered negative because it was associated with

pain and fear. What are pain and fear? Emotions, exactly. Do you know that emotions have the power to literally "fix" mental programs that are implemented again and automatically every time the same stimulation occurs? The stronger the emotion we associate with a circumstance, a place, a person, etc., the stronger and more rooted our mind's perception of it will be. Some talk about cellular memory, that is, a memory contained in our cells, in this case the brain, which become like the keys on a piano. You touch them (ideally) and they give you the same note over and over again, unless you can change the pitch of the stroke associated with that key. It's a complicated concept, but I think I've made it accessible to most people, as I said I'm not a therapist, so despite having a good knowledge of the human mind and body I don't intend to make a sort of treatise on psychology, as I said in the preface I want just sharing my experience and that of other people on the topic. My intent is precisely to make you change the intonation of certain notes just enough to accelerate your liberation. Already the fact of knowing that I was not the only one who had known Panico and his visits was a source of relief for me at the time. Is this the case for you too? As I have already said, I was ashamed to say that I had panic attacks... for many reasons largely due to my psychological profile and my character. Realizing that I wasn't the only one this happened to represented an important lever. It's as if I had discovered that I was carrying the weight of this boulder together with millions of people, even famous ones, so feeling part of something made me trigger the lever to lift the boulder. Giving back my experience to anyone who finds benefit from it gratifies me on a human level. This arises from an awareness that occurred in the months following the end of my meetings with Panico. Get ready because now we enter the field of maximum systems. Oh I know, balls... allow me to do it for a few lines. Then we pick up the thread again. In what I called my midlife crisis I reflected on the meaning of life (thanks to Panico). I asked myself, beyond the religious and spiritual beliefs that concern the soul and its infinite nature, what remains of a man's life at the end? Everything he has learned, everything he has understood, is it useful or has it been useful only to him or can it be useful to others? Isn't this associated with the progress of humanity and its evolution? Ergo. We all know the stories or discoveries of so-called famous people, doctors, scientists, researchers and so on... each of them has left us something written, something from which to draw either to move forward or to go further. Have you ever wondered what would have happened if Guglielmo Marconi had erased his discoveries and made wireless only for his house? How will we be placed now?

Someone in the years to come from those discoveries, from those foundations, built something more advanced. Therefore, leaving a trace of us can be considered as the piece of a puzzle that we, each of us, puts into the great puzzle of humanity. Based on this reasoning, I also write about a topic like others. Not on the basis of academic studies, but on the basis of my experience and the readings that I have done out of personal culture to help me overcome a wall. Knowledge is a set of many ladders that are stored here and there, ready to be used when needed. I have an obstacle on the path, it's a wall, it's called Panic, I go online and look for the pieces to assemble the ladder that I will climb to climb over that wall. End. Based on this assumption I like to think that this track will help someone in their time of need. When I needed it, I found the traces of others who had followed certain paths before me, in various fields, and I realized that thanks to the work of others, from time to time, I was able to evolve and advance, and as I already mentioned I want to return the favor. One could object that by now everything is already there, and I partially agree because everything we have is missing what we still have to discover, but in general it is true that in the last two decades healthy technology has connected us in such a great enough to be able to glimpse the puzzle of humanity in a broader way, for better or for worse.

But the same topic explained by different people changes in the way it is perceived. The concept that perhaps I cannot express is similar to the concept of repetitions at school. That is to say. Professor X explains the mathematics to me, let's pretend, the equations. I don't understand anything unlike my classmates. I decide to pay another doctor to do the repetitions. So I discover that my mind, which had not understood a topic explained by Tizio, is able to understand it explained by Caio. The topic is the same, my mind is the same and yet..and yet. So maybe a therapist follows you, maybe you found some advice on the internet, and despite this you don't get out of it, Panic keeps coming back, good. I want to believe that by reading this book which offers a different perspective on the phenomenon, perhaps you will be able to see the topic in a different way, no longer as a problem but as a solution.

Let's get back to us then. We were saying that Panic enters our lives in two ways: either with a sudden and unexpected trauma or following ignored accumulations of Anxiety and Stress. For the first case I shared Elisa's experience, for the second case I share Diego's story.

Diego is a specialized worker and since his high school days he has lived with Anxiety and Stress which began to visit him after failing his second year at technical institute. Before then he had never had to deal with these symptoms. The person we are talking about at the time was very sunny, joyful, very good at playing football but evidently with a great sensitivity quite covered by a Gascon attitude. A boy therefore apparently very self-confident. But adolescence for everyone is a very delicate moment, during which the emotional impact of certain events becomes amplified and risks marking you for life, also because the mind is extremely receptive and the structure is largely virgin because it is nourished from a low level of experiences and situations that are confined by protected environments such as school, family, sport. The second year of high school, thanks to frequenting companies made up of kids with little desire to do anything, led him to fail. In the following year, this event generated the onset of stress psoriasis which appeared on the hands every time tests and homework were carried out in class. In his unconscious the fear of failure grew silently but he warned it at the same time with signals visible to the naked eye. He arrived at the state exam ignoring everything. On this occasion psoriasis also appeared on his feet. The fact of seeing these stains accentuated his anxiety and forced him to explain to anyone who saw it what it was due to. He passed the exam, thank God, and started working almost immediately. He thought that everything was over now, there were no more exams, there were no more grades, he felt free. However, since exams never end, from time to time even at work, on the occasion of business trips and at the beginning of each new job Anxiety and Stress returned to visit him. His way of keeping them at bay was weekend entertainment, those mini holidays that unconsciously represented the end of school. On holidays everything disappeared as if by magic. Then he started changing jobs every two years, blaming the episodes of stress either on his colleagues or on his boss. So between ups and downs he postponed his appointment with himself. He should have reworked that failure from many years ago in his mind and accepted it in his mind as something that can happen to anyone and which in any case was a consequence of the fact that he didn't commit himself. In short, he lived with the unconscious belief that he was not good enough and with the fear of making mistakes. The focus of his mind was always on the fear of making mistakes. The constant fear of being rejected again, and therefore every new job, every new love story started badly and ended worse and the anxiety rose every time, because every time his conviction of not being up to it was strengthened. So one fine day Panico arrived to teach him that he could no longer live in fear of making mistakes, because the more he tried not to make mistakes the more he made them due to anxiety, it's called self-sabotage. In him it manifested itself in a similar way to mine, therefore difficulty breathing, great fear and difficulty controlling his arms and legs. He spent a year with treatments based on homeopathic products and the practice of Yoga. So his way out was a little different from Elisa's, let's say softer. However, even for him who has a similar story to mine, when certain situations arise that reveal Stress and Anxiety, the fear of the return of Panic leads him to immediately find his balance. Another metaphor that I feel like using regarding Panico and his cousins is the one that represents them as warning lights on the dashboard of the car. Ignoring them over time can lead to forced blocks, while facing them distances us from the traumatic event. As I have already argued, once Panic arrives to get you out of the cage you have created for yourself it doesn't go away immediately, it waits for you to move away from the prison until you are at a safe distance. You can't cheat. I myself, after going straight for two years, find myself hosting him albeit in a soft way these days. So I stopped to ask myself questions. The answer is that for two weeks the level of anxiety and stress has suddenly increased following the onset of some recent events which have once again stimulated certain moods. However, having corrected the intonation of certain notes, I know very well what to do, and above all I don't let myself be caught unprepared. I share my case certain that some of the readers have the same profile as me. I'm a planner, who likes to schedule everything. According to some therapists, this attitude is a form of control aimed unconsciously at avoiding anxiety. I admit I'm aware of it. When you plan something and there are no surprises everything runs smoothly. Unexpected events, in the form of problems, never warn you. The attitude with which you face them makes the difference. Staying centered, taking a deep breath and calmly accepting and dealing with them is the correct way to resolve the issue, whatever it may be. Getting agitated, trying to postpone, brooding, getting angry, on the other hand, leads to two consequences. Not solving the problem and in the case of predisposed individuals like me, accumulating anxiety and stress which, if ignored, give way to panic. I let my guard down, in other words, and let myself be carried away by negative emotions. Now what happens? The cellular memory sensed those notes of anger, nervousness and frustration so to get out of it it generated a sort of alarm. The alarm activated my allies. It's time to stop for a while in the free moments of the day and address the issue. Here I start to tell you about the techniques I use to avoid face to face with Panic which would lead to slowdowns that I prefer to avoid. I know that when he arrives it's like having a guest in the house, it's not like you can throw him out as you want and whenever you want, so let's say he's in the garden, he's not in the house. To get it back I follow some steps.

The first thing I do is use internal dialogue and analyze events. What made me angry? That person, that situation etc. at this stage it goes without saying that you must not cheat. Lying to yourself, not giving the right weight to something is the best way to make the situation worse. Have you ever heard the phrase "learn to live in the world?" here I say to myself: -"learn to live in the world!" - if you have a problem it's your problem, no one will come to save you, nothing outside will come to your aid simply because you create your reality. When you are centered, external reality is the fruit of your internal balance, when you experience discomfort it is because you are the generator. So you project that frequency outside of yourself by experiencing it. Accepting this perspective means that you assume responsibility for everything that happens to you. Blaming others, circumstances or even the world is easy, stupid but above all deresponsible. That's why Panico returns.

How have I been behaving lately?

How did I evaluate this or that situation?

Have I still made the same errors in judgment, behavior, etc.? Yes. Well. How do I resolve the situation? Changing my mental and emotional approach. Rework the situation. Rewrite the story of that episode without associating negative emotions or negative notes with it. The expression comes to mind - "drowning in a glass of water" - translated as making an unexpected event a huge tragedy. I gave the wrong weight to situations that had much, much, much less weight than they did. Why does this happen? Or rather when does this happen? When we don't feel good about ourselves. I go into detail to make you understand the practical application in my life.

Chapter 3

"Overestimate yourself thinking you can solve it without self-analysis"

Since I was a child I have shown intolerance for certain rules. Not for everyone. I was an obedient child, but if I wanted to do something and was

prevented from doing so, I had a very hard time accepting it. This occasionally led me to clashes with my father's authority. An old-fashioned parental figure. Very authoritarian, like:
-"No, because it's no, or not because I say so! And that's that"-
So not receiving logical explanations or motivations that I could understand sent my nervous system into haywire. In response to these rare but constant situations over the years, I implemented rebellious behaviors that rooted in my mind an "action-reaction" mechanism that was very difficult to defuse. In fact, at the dawn of forty years of age, if I have to do something that I don't understand or that doesn't make logical sense to my way of reasoning, that movement of rebellion from time to time accumulates in a sort of emotional tank that sooner or later it fills up. If then what I had disputed turns out to be correct in the objection that I had a priori brought to someone's attention...then I explode and assert my reasons. The emotional tank becomes a pressure cooker and begins to whistle and chug steam. I hate being right in other words. This attitude determines the union of "emotional ingredients" which, mixing over a certain time, determine the onset of anxiety and stress. These two gentlemen enter me when I have to actually accept what I don't want to accept, when I have to repress something.

How does this modus operandi reverberate in my life?

In relationships I simply close relationships especially if they are with people who are not important to me, in other words I choose not to deal with them to avoid discomfort. This is very important. Knowing how to recognize what bothers us and free ourselves from it. With people who are important to me, therefore family and friends, I express my disappointment in the appropriate manner and generally let it go.

In working life, however, it is often very difficult to distance oneself from a boss or colleague who impacts the nervous system. We must quickly try to find a solution for peaceful living through dialogue and civil confrontation, balancing the situations from time to time. Once you keep the point by justifying your choice, another time you give way and bite the bullet. By doing so you learn to be in the world.

If unfortunately I happen to deal with a manager who shows authoritarianism then things change. Why? Because of my nature, because of what I am, and of what I am aware, the intolerance of impositions. So it's not the fault of authoritarian people that I feel intolerance within me, they are like that, it's their essence, it's neither right nor wrong. There are people who are temperamentally compatible with this type of subject and

incompatible people. So what do I do every time I have to deal with these people? I tolerate it as long as I can. It is I who choose to face an epilogue that I know well. In my last work experience for example, after a month I changed a manager. From above they had imposed a character who had a profile incompatible with mine.
Not having to deal with it directly, and having an idyllic relationship with all the colleagues including the three supervisors, I didn't give it any weight. But every time I was forced to deal with it, I felt the typical annoyance which then disappeared as I continued working. The fact is that after a year having to choose whether to continue or not knowing what I would face in the famous "variable period of time" I decided not to continue. The resulting disappointment led to the emergence of a year of accumulation, the sadness of leaving magnificent colleagues and the awareness of having to start all over again. This mix was the basis on which Ansia rested. Putting the ninety load on it at a time like this came with unexpected mechanical work and the flooding of the cellar which I had to clear out. This is why Panico returns. I had a bad series of events and was locking myself in a cage. So he came to save me again, hence the input to write this book. I bring this recent example to highlight in practice what I mean by self-analysis. Obviously I didn't do it in

these two days but three years ago. The awareness of myself, the analysis of my experience with a therapist and with my readings allowed me to already have the solution in my pocket. I'm not saying it's easy, but compared to three years ago I know who I'm dealing with and how to handle it. Three years ago it wasn't like this. As I have already mentioned, I tried to solve it myself when I was a lorry driver. I tried to control my mind using DIY autogenic training and motivation techniques. I neglected to have a problem until I couldn't hide anymore. I remember once, I stopped at a service station because I felt the sensations that preceded the panic attack, having now become accustomed to it, I knew when it started and how, so I thought of stopping, waiting twenty minutes and leaving again. But unfortunately for me another colleague had also stopped at the same service station and therefore I couldn't do my breathing exercises. We got the coffee and set off again, but immediately after leaving the service station which for me represented a temporary life buoy, the spasms started again... I couldn't do anything but pull over to the emergency lane and wait for the end, but the colleague who He had seen that I had pulled over and called me immediately to make sure of my condition. I found it hard to speak but, lying to him and to myself, I told him I had to tie my shoe and hung up the phone. After five minutes I resumed my normal working day. In that period Panico understood, as an intelligent entity, that I was a tough nut to crack. He was no longer able to take total control of my mind because I had become good at anticipating and recognizing it, furthermore while the attack was happening I repeated to myself - "it's just Panic that wants to greet you today too" - therefore the very annoying thoughts related to death imminent they were no longer created. I cushioned the blow and set off again. I went on like this for about a year. At the rate of one or two episodes a week. You get used to it I thought. But it was a haughty attitude. It is undeniable that I used effective mental techniques independently as a self-taught person but I continued to stubbornly remain in a work environment that I could no longer stand, this was the truth. I was feeling sick and therefore 'vibrated' at an uncomfortable frequency, and the discomfort obviously resonated. After that year, 2021, the now desperate Panic raised the intensity of his interventions and since he mentally could no longer fool me, he involved the second mind that all humans have. The one in the intestine. Oh yeah, maybe you knew, or maybe not. However, in the intestine it is also a common thought among many doctors, that a kind of emotional second brain resides. So I started having very bad gastritis, which didn't go away with common medications. I then decided to finally turn to my doctor, who understood that if the stomach medications didn't work, the problem wasn't physical but of another nature. He told me about work stress, but I turned a deaf ear and downplayed it. I went on for another six months until one morning I got into my vehicle, traveled about ten kilometers and was no longer able to continue, I left the motorway but I couldn't pull over onto the ring road so I slowed down to a crawl, unleashing everyone's anger. the drivers sounding like enraged lunatics. Then I saw a service area, a petrol station and I stopped there. I knew I couldn't continue the day, I was writhing like a worm due to stomach spasms, I had to go back to the company. So I called, said I felt unwell, and walked back. I had to go to hospital. They did the tests as usual and everything was within the parameters. They gave me two days of rest, even in that case I omitted to mention that I was subject to panic attacks. While I was on the hospital bed waiting for the results of the blood tests and the visit I had done, I started with the internal dialogue, telling myself that everything was ok, that I just needed a little time off and that I would go back to work on Monday. Yet inside me it was exactly what I didn't want. So I implemented another technique, that of silence. This technique consists in a few words, in silencing the little voice that we all have in our heads, the voice of thoughts. You need a calm place, preferably while lying down or sitting, and consists of creating a vacuum in the mind to essentially calm it down. Absence of thoughts, calm, quiet, relaxation. I was alone in the room so I could easily do it. This exercise, which seems easy, is successful for beginners for about ten seconds, then undergoes interruptions and with practice you can achieve tens of minutes of absence of thoughts. It's a real lifesaver but its effectiveness varies depending on the circumstances. It is very useful in neuroses, when two hundred thoughts are spinning in your mind, usually fueled by anxiety. After a few minutes however, after a bit of silence in my mind a thought came from that little voice. A question. "Is this where you want to stay?" reported to the hospital. And he continued. -"This is the second time you find yourself in hospital, how many more times do you intend to find yourself in this situation? Do you think it will always be okay? That you'll get away with it every time? You know what you have to do, you have to leave this job" - I knew it very well even if I pretended nothing happened, but it seemed crazy to me. It wasn't the time. All the pandemic madness was going on, companies weren't hiring, many were closed due to the lockdown... only a madman could leave his job. So logic prohibited me from taking that step. So I left the hospital convinced that I would go back to work, and the more I thought about Monday the more Anxiety spread on my chest, Panic was there ready to intervene. Monday arrives, I go down to the kitchen where I had prepared my backpack with work things, I drink coffee, smoke a cigarette, go to the bathroom and then go down to leave. Or at least I thought I was leaving. Now you'll think I'm crazy. I couldn't lift my backpack. I was stuck. It's called "Burnout". A new character in this story. My combative nature didn't accept the other three, let alone if I could accept this one. But now after two years of fighting I had reached my limit, I no longer had the strength to fight but I didn't want to give up. Surrender is not in my value system. But I always had my logic. And this one told me that if I didn't agree to stop there would be nothing good waiting for me. Because if Anxiety, Stress and Panic fail to make you stop for a moment or the time it takes to get you back into balance, characters arrive that I don't care to get to know. They are called exhaustion and depression. With them the level definitely rises and there is very little to joke about. The consequences for many are very serious. I therefore wanted to avoid the subsequent steps. So I had to admit to myself that alone, despite the readings, despite the techniques, I was no longer able to manage the situation, I had to raise the white flag. A heavy blow to my ego and my presumption of the time. I didn't go to work that day, I called, went to the doctor and got another sick day. I hadn't announced my resignation, I was desperately clinging to the thought that maybe, with another day off, I could carry on. But no. In the afternoon Panico came to visit me and shook me with a certain intensity. I was alone at home lying in bed. I couldn't make him stop. I knew there was only one way to make it stop. Call the company and resign. So, not having the strength to speak, I wrote a message to the managers saying that I could no longer work and to go on holiday until I was fired for which two weeks and communication from the INPS was needed. It may seem incredible but after sending that text everything disappeared. I was free, I was out of the cage, now I just had to walk away. I found another temporary job for a month, then when the contract expired I decided to take advantage of unemployment, something I had never done but which was the only way to have time and some money, not a lot, but enough to pay the mortgage and expenses. What mattered most, however, was time for me and with me. I turned to a very good psychologist and for a year, once a week I went to get assistance in my work of internal reconstruction. The work on yourself must be done alone even if you go to a psychologist. These figures, like guardians, assist us to get up, they explain to us as much as possible why we have fallen but then we have to take the steps to advance alone, one foot in front of the other, each at her own pace. In the first session I even started crying, something I hadn't done for twenty years. All this arose from the question: -"what's happening?" - and I had a lot to tell, there was a lot of material in that emotional tank that had overflowed. During the therapy I actually self-analyzed my entire more or less recent life, digging deep and unraveling the tangled mess that had been tangled up for years in which it was never the right time. Panic disappears forever or rather until the day before yesterday. Now I know the path to take.

Chapter 4

"Failing to have a problem"

Omission. Because it happens. For fear. Fear of what? Perhaps the judgment of others? Maybe to show weakness? Yes, all these things. For others more, for others less. In subjects in need of consideration and approval from others, as a form of nourishment to strengthen self-esteem, this is absolutely not a problem, in fact asking for help is a way to let the world know that they exist. There's nothing bad. It's just a way of being. The ways of being, as I said for subjects inclined towards authoritarianism, are what they are and I do not make a judgment regarding this. Therefore, if showing your weaknesses is the vehicle for building or strengthening social interactions, it is not a problem to ask for help. For everyone else, getting help is almost unnatural behavior and therefore creates discomfort. Shame is a form of fear. More subtle, but no less incisive. From my experience, shame of something or for something is linked to thought forms inherent to judgment and the appearance of oneself. I would also add the principles of social conformity that determine approval. Conventions, the basic ideas of society that shapes itself following the administration of certain models that create standards. These standards tend to make you identify with them. What are the standards of the society you live in? In my society, the Western one, the standards of the "good" are connected to concepts such as respect for rules, success, work and family. Until a few years ago, the stereotype of the strong man was very fashionable. This stereotype brought to exasperation by the mass media and social conventions, through the models proposed in cinematography, literature, entertainment and so on, reached its maximum, its peak until around the beginning of the 2000s in a crescendo which started in the 1930s and has capitulated in the present day. In summary I am talking about the myth of the hero. You may say, but what does this have to do with panic attacks? It has to do with the extent to which your existential parameters are incorrectly calibrated by what surrounds you and which also and above all determines your state of mind without you realizing it. So allow me to freely continue this reasoning and stay focused on the common thread. Then we will talk about techniques for dealing with, communicating with and greeting Panic when it arrives. However, if you find the following lines tedious you can skip directly to the next chapter "Techniques for communicating with Panic".

I was talking about the models created by society to ensure that they were imitated and the ultimately disastrous consequences that they produced. So what are these harmful effects? The annihilation of man. Now if you give me so much by reproducing the same path on women we will witness the annihilation of women in the times to come. I will explain this consideration briefly. As you know, I'm almost forty years old so I come from the eighties. When I was a child, television was the only means of communication besides the radio and in the early nineties the prevailing narrative or story-telling was that of the strong man, at the cinema they showed films like "Rambo" "Rocky" ' 'Robocop" "Pretty Woman" and so on, in one way or another the reference model was that of an invincible, successful man who managed to do everything even save the world. But what a beautiful thing... yes everything is beautiful, but those standards of great wealth, of great strength then in the daily reality of the vast majority of men were a little different. Stereotypes such as "the hunter man who brings bread home" "the career man who changes his life and buys a villa with a swimming pool" the self-made man" etc. they unconsciously constituted an ideal for the masses to strive for which however was impossible to achieve. Let's be clear, I'm not saying impossible because I have low levels of self-esteem or because I don't think it's possible to change one's life for the better, humanly, professionally, physically, etc. I define it as impossible in the sense that it cannot be like this for everyone. Ergo. Let's imagine for a moment that we are all successful men, all great entrepreneurs, all great athletes, all owners of luxury goods. Well. Would be great. Yes. Um... please... I mean, who would work for these successful entrepreneurs? Who would build the luxury homes? Who would work in a factory to make the cars we should all drive? eh..evidently there is and was something wrong with this reasoning. "The man who never has to ask" do you remember this slogan? A do-it-all man who could basically accomplish anything short of fathering children. That's why there were women, the custodians of the home, the housewives who raised

children and took care of the house, etc. After
about thirty years more and more people realized
that those models were not possible for everyone,
therefore the sense of inadequacy, of failure, of
failure, of deprivation began to take root in many
minds, fortunately not in all, and to generate the
inadequacy that led to the collapse of the society.
Today we work but not with all jobs we can be
independent. So you go judged, "at forty years old
still at home with your parents" ah, what a
shame...shame of what?.."eh you have to make
sacrifices, work your way up, it takes time..." look
at it average salary, the type of precarious or
permanent contract and the salary level and you
compare it to the cost of living and you realize that
something isn't right. When does modern man go
into crisis in this narrative? When he sees that he
cannot do what his father or grandfather even
managed to do. Therefore the comparison with
one's peers becomes apparently unsustainable. I say
apparently because the conditions are not the same
but no one pays attention to this. The parameters
and opportunities are extremely different.
However, it was enough to introduce the idea of
failure combined with a sense of guilt to cause
social structures and certainties to collapse. The
house is no longer a certainty, much less a right,
you can forget about your pension, your job is no
longer permanent, and so on. At the same time, my

friend, the cards on the table change, the paradigm apparently changes, but the script that tends to keep your mood low after having drugged you with illusions is always the same. Now the model to follow, the new diktat is: The strong woman. oh..the strength of women, the power of women, career women, the working mother, the woman in politics, the President, the wonder-woman... it's her. You see her? The first female Premier? Do you see the great Entrepreneur? Do you see the first Presidenta? Do you, my friend, want to be less? Don't you also think you can do what she did? Go ahead... aspire to this model, this is your future, you deserve more. Divorce your husband, she will pay your alimony! And you will be able to emancipate yourself with a new job... stop. Stop. Don't listen to him. Your husband earns 1400 euros a month and you have a 700 euro mortgage and car payments plus bills, the children's school and everything else. So if you want to break up with him due to financial problems, know that you won't have a good life anyway, if he's in trouble now, imagine later. If the problem is a relationship one, that's another thing but we'll talk about it later. Don't listen to him, don't get fooled like us men got fooled. You are worthy of love and consideration even if you don't become President of something or some parliament, you are worthy of love and consideration even if you do cleaning in the black.

If you use these reference models, life will always be unsatisfactory and anxiety and stress will arrive faster and more widely and if you are unlucky, Panic will also arrive. I'm not the one saying that the consumption of anxiolytics and antidepressants has increased. But what I tell you is that the antidepressant or anxiolytic is inside you. Find your balance in your essence not in the false myths that are offered. You have nothing to envy of any other woman. The same goes for you man. If you don't drive a 100,000 euro car you're still fine, if you're not the president of something you're still fine, if you're not self-made and have a fixed-term contract and live with your parents because the banks won't let you the mortgage, doesn't mean you're not a hero. All this seems disconnected from the emotion that then generates the problems we face and that I face. Instead, in my very humble opinion it is all connected at a subtle level. Then Anxiety, Stress and Panic are no longer pathologies, they are friends who intervene in your life to remind you of who and what you are. My love. We love you just as you are. Whoever you are, whatever you do, my love we love you. Nobody asks you to prove anything. We know what they did to you, we know how much you suffered, we know who let you down and how, but listen to us. Live and love. Fuck you!!!. Well.

Now after this macro-social reasoning let's return to us and our friends. In the next chapter I will try to suggest some techniques that I used to overcome the various moments of the relationship with Panic. I will suggest techniques to help you notice the signs that announce his arrival after he shows up for the first time, other techniques for communicating with your deepest self in the subsequent phases and precautions to be implemented in the times that follow when he leaves. Receiving these suggestions does not give you any guarantee that they will be useful to you. But at least try. Some of these techniques involve mental visualization. no. It's not science fiction or something abstract, you can do it. It goes without saying that it is up to you, to the commitment you will make, to the sincerity with which you will analyze your very respectable personal vicissitudes, which are yours and no one else's. Then, based on the techniques, I will try to provide you with examples, the "case histories" of the people who have shared their panicked experiences with me. We could start a club, "panic fans".

Chapter 5

"Techniques for communicating with Panic"

Well found, my friend, whether you have read the
end of the previous chapter or whether you have
skipped the "sermon" of considerations that I
defined as macro-social. Well.
So let's talk about some techniques that, as I say,
are used to communicate with Panic. Please note
that I do not use terms like cope, cure etc.
I asked you to make an effort to completely
overturn your perspective, or the perspective that
they imposed on you, I asked you to stop seeing it
as a problem, I asked you to imagine it as any
being, you choose whether to give it human form,
animal, vegetable or abstract. View it. Then go
back to visualizing your space as I explained at the
beginning. If you, your mind, were a shape, what
shape would it be? How is this space of yours? Are
there fences? Are there walls? Where does Panic
come from? What does your prison represent?
Where have you locked yourself up? In a job? In a
relationship? In solitude? In empty friendships? In
dissatisfaction? In defeats? What takes your breath
away? When does Panic arrive? At night? At
morning? At work? At home? Process, focus my
love. Yes, I know, I'm asking a lot of you, I'm
bombarding you with questions, I'm messing up

your synapses on neural networks... what are
synapses and neural networks? Leave it now,
maybe I'll explain it to you later. I want you to
focus, I want you to look him in the eyes, I want
you to think back to your first meeting. I want you
to describe me and describe the details to yourself.
It was hot? it was cold? What clothes were you
wearing? Let me remind you, try hard...
Excellent, excellent.
Focus… one more moment…. Breathe...inhale and
exhale, blocking one nostril, do it three times...
so...very good..
now I want you to make an effort to identify the
path that took you there, to that meeting with him.
Was it a traumatic event like for Elisa? Or did you
get there little by little by repressing yourself? By
dint of swallowing toads...think, reflect...
Breathe in...breathe...again...
let's begin..
The first technique, as you may have guessed,
concerns breathing. You can find everything on the
subject on the internet, some explanations are
understandable, others are clearly invented because
it is fashionable, others are too complicated to
apply in those moments. The web is full of
consultants, therapists and the like who have never
met him in person, they rely on readings, on
definitions of medical literature which is fine let's
be clear, but it's one thing to read what others have

written, it's another thing to live it. Do you agree with me? Well.
I will therefore explain two techniques that I have used successfully. The first concerns breathing through one nostril. The second is reverse breathing.

Breathe with one nostril

This technique, extremely effective as you have already understood, involves blocking one nostril with the finger, exerting light pressure with the index finger on the nostril to close it, leaving the other free.

The moment Panico arrives for a visit, this gesture must automatically be triggered, which also involves the sense of touch. Involving the senses in the peak moment of the event is in itself another technique which I will mention later. Well. Now to ensure that you learn this technique you have to train. You must prepare your body to correctly implement this sequence of movements as if it were a sacred and magical ritual. So make yourself comfortable and try this exercise. Head straight, gently close one nostril and breathe only with the other, do this for four to five breaths then change nostril. It's a very simple operation. By learning it mechanically as soon as the fateful encounter happens, wherever you are you can do it. You will pretend to be out of breath, you will go into tachycardia and you will know that he has decided to stop by and say hello. Immediately place your finger on your nostril and breathe counting from 1 to 5 and then from 5 to 1. Then change your nostril. The effectiveness of this technique is given by the combination of the conscious use, therefore control, of breathing and the use of touch. Why is it important to control yourself and touch something? Because as you know, in those moments Panic enters your head, and the thoughts you hear are his teasing him, the human mind, easily deceived, believes it is she who is speaking, but no, instead it is him. So by implementing controlled breathing and activating conscious touch you take part of the control, and this is especially important the first few times. Panic is impetuous and tends to push you down a slope, which is why he accelerates your heartbeat and even gives you tremors. What you do in this metaphor is apply a handbrake, or a fingerbrake. You have to imagine that the gesture of plugging the nostril is actually the handbrake button. You can't stop him from pushing you but you can stop him from picking up speed. He accelerates, you brake. Simple right? If you know volleyball, using another metaphor, he tries to crush, you block him and neutralize him by mitigating his strength. These reactions of yours will discourage him. He plays pranks on you, he's a joker. He enjoys seeing you disoriented and scared, the more you get scared, the more you shit yourself and the more he laughs. There are people like that, they play pranks and enjoy seeing them succeed, but if you learn to ruin the joke, you will transfer the frustration onto him who will be happy anyway. Because the stronger you become, the weaker he

becomes. You remember what I told you at the beginning of the book that when he acts undisturbed the power ratio between him and you is 10 to 1? and do you remember what else I told you? That I will take you by the hand to overturn the ratio, transforming it into 1 to 10.
Well. Now if you manage to stop it, or even just mitigate it and reduce the time it stays, the ratio already becomes 8 to 3.
he is still ahead, but he has already lost 2 points, while you have gained them. Take and bring home. YOU WIN!
Using this technical basis, the next step if you can automate one-nostril breathing is to use your internal dialogue. If you speak in your mind, he doesn't speak. He remembers that your mind is your own. It's your space. You're in charge. Then you will take care of understanding how he arrived at the self-analysis which we then take up again as a concept. So let's assume, he arrives suddenly. He starts telling you that you're having a heart attack, or that you're generally going to die, or he tells you to call an ambulance because you're having an attack of something. You have already started breathing with one nostril and counting: 1,2,3,4,5 – 5,4,3,2,1.
He now begins to respond to that voice. Talk to us. Use the following sentences:
-"I discovered you, go away, it's not the time"

-"it's still you, you're monotonous"
-"don't you ever get bored, loser?"
-" Still? Everyone knows you by now."
They are four little sentences, unconventional I know. But the conventional ones you can read from others. From those who copy what others have written without ever having tried it. I don't teach you to sing in playback, I teach you to go on stage live, my love. Let's Rock
Panico likes to be recognized and even insulted, he is very sorry when you spoil his performances, but deep down he is happy for you, because the more you advance and move away from the cage to chase him, the more he retreats. That's why it's there, always remember it. He is taking you out of that hole where you are holed up for X reasons. When you are far enough away from the cage he will flee so far that you will no longer be able to see him even with a telescope, as long as you don't make the same mistakes throughout your life. I ask you and he asks you for courage. Come out, you are a chosen one. Not everyone deserves to be saved. Not everyone is warned before the abyss. You have the great, immense fortune of being among the chosen. He chose to get you out of trouble. "Those who know everything" define it as an inconvenience that comes suddenly. They use big words... they practice academics. But they don't

know what they're talking about, so far we understand each other.

And we understood that Panic comes as a result of two and only two reasons. Either due to a sudden trauma which then activates it, or due to a series of situations which accumulate in your "emotional tank" as I say, Anxiety and Stress, his two cousins. You will see that if before reading this book Panico's caresses lasted 20-30-40 minutes, by becoming master of yourself in that moment, thanks to one-nostril breathing, the sensorial stimulation of touch and internal dialogue you will at least halve the duration of the caresses. his visits. Well.

Reverse breathing

Now let's see the other breathing technique, this is a little more complex to use when encountering Panic because it requires skills that you will only acquire with practice. However, it is very useful to ward off what they call anticipatory anxiety. When does Miss Anxiety turn anticipatory? When panic attacks become associated in your mind with a place, a situation or a person. Generally this happens following the first episode of your soap opera. In my case, in a car, and in a very specific point on the motorway where it had happened for the first time. After that point it disappeared. It is therefore possible if it happened to you at work or at home, that when you have to face the situation, place or person that bothers you, you unconsciously call it out. But since you don't know where to find him, your only contact, your only intermediary with her is her cousin Ansia, who is called to carry out a function that belongs to her and not to her. She comes to annoy you to make you understand that that situation isn't good for you, you usually ignore her, repress her with drugs or by running away from situations, so she doesn't act as an intermediary for Panico, she doesn't work for him. She only calls him when you don't want to listen to her, are we there? Well.

This is more or less what happens here. You start thinking about the moment you have to face, the

place you have to go. Right? In your mind you then press a button. Do you remember the keys and tunings that I explained to you before? Well. So you know that when you press that button, what happens? Or rather what do you make happen? Exact. That key produces that note, that frequency that in your mind you have associated with a strong and negative emotion that is linked to that circumstance. You stimulate the memory of the pain and you start to be afraid of being afraid. And you start producing that frequency, and what attracts that frequency? Anxiety. Who shows up for the appointment because you keep pressing that blessed button. You become Anxiety. When she comes into your mind because you keep calling her, she realizes you missed the note. It's like you get the wrong phone number on a call. You call with the belief that Panic will answer and instead Anxiety answers. And what does she tell you? She tells you that you have the wrong number. And then you reply that you are looking for Panic. And she very politely says to you: -"I'll pass it on to you straight away"-
And he reveals himself, he doesn't talk to you right away. She understands that you want to meet him and she tells you:-"I'll wait for you there, in the usual place"-
So when you get to the moment or the point or in front of the person, he is ready and puts himself in

command of your mind long enough for him to have a laugh at seeing you in that condition. Are you afraid of Panic? You're afraid of being afraid. Do you know why? Because up until today you've taken them by storm. In every game with him you have always lost without putting up any resistance, without reacting and therefore your self-esteem is below sea level, you are under water. It's as if they invited you to play a tennis match, but before entering the court they either don't give you the racket or they tie it with a rope behind your back. Can you play without a racket? No my love. Yet the match starts anyway, everyone in the stadium watches you while you take ball after ball in the face and lose self-esteem points, someone even laughs at you. They tell you that you just want attention, that you are not strong enough. That there are those who are worse off. If you are a man and you don't save the world then... it's your fault, if you're a woman and you're not President of something it's always your fault, the others make it. It's just that I've never liked injustices, I'll give you the racket, dear love. Let's be clear, it's not like you win right away now, you have to learn to play. But at least you have the tools to compete. At least if not all, but some balls you start hitting them and scoring some points. We are starting to close the gap. Let's at least start by not hitting them in the face. Well.

What does reverse breathing mean? I'll explain it to you right away but I need you. I want you to take a deep breath and place your attention on your body, especially your belly and chest. Now, inhaling deeply should make your belly swell, or your chest swell. Generally, shortness of breath occurs in the chest, after an effort or a run or if we get agitated, in normal things without high emotions the air goes into the belly which inflates and deflates like a balloon, right? I then want you to start focusing on your belly. If you lie down, it is better if you sit, place the palm of your hand over your navel and inhale, inflating your belly as much as you can. Inhale and inflate, exhale and deflate. You are here? Well.

Now I want you to take control of this involuntary movement. I want you to inhale and as you do so draw your belly in, as if you were doing a swimsuit test and wanted to cheat. Inhale and pull your belly in. Exhale and push your belly out. Reverse breathing indeed. This type of technique is very useful for relaxation, and since as you know the belly is also a second brain, with this technique applied for two to three minutes you can obtain a great benefit. If this is easy for you, then when Panic comes to visit you, place one hand on your belly like you just did and start doing reverse breathing. This will focus your mind on an action, your controlled breathing, and again on touch.

Your hand brought by you to a very specific
position.
The phrases you can use here, when doing this
technique are as follows:
-"It's not up to me"
-"it's just Panico who wants to say hello to me"
-"I'll split the package without the heel"
-" He snores and knocks without passing"
As I suggested, you can use this technique before
facing the situation, when you feel the preventive
discomfort that generates anticipatory anxiety.
At the beginning it is obvious that you will
continue to press that key that gives you this note.
It is an action-reaction mechanism that you have
ingrained and overwritten in your mind following
the defeats you have suffered on the field every
time you felt helpless. You were alone without a
racket baby. Now you have it and you have to learn
to use it. You must train yourself to dissociate the
negative emotion from the place or situation in the
PAST where the first episode occurred. In one
word darling: rework. Which is different from
reliving. You don't have to relive anything at all,
it's already happened, it's already passed, it's gone,
now you're here, you're with me. So be careful not
to make a fatal mistake. Stay in the cage. The next
chapter.

Chapter 6

"Gct out of the cage!"

Having reached this point my darling, you have
understood that before you were defenseless or
with ineffective or insufficient defenses while now
you have two to use. We will see the others shortly,
but I intend to make sure that you have become
aware of the fact that you are no longer unarmed.
This awareness is fundamental, because now,
bringing you another example on my specific case,
I want you, after a bit of practice, to go and look for
it. Yes, he usually comes whenever he wants, he

ambushes you to scare you, he makes fun of you. This time we're going to pick him up at home. He wants you to chase him. Because he knows that if you chase him you will move away from the cage. Have you ever seen a car chase? Of the police in the movies? Or in the jungle? How does this happen exactly? Did you notice? View.

There is one who chases and one who is chased, right? Well.

There is a moment in which there is an exchange of glances between the two, then there is a moment of silence, then the chase starts, then they take off...right? Well.

Also remember my darling that Panic, in our paradigm is a friend and an ally who has come to free us from the prison we have built for ourselves with the invisible bars of Anxiety and Stress and various ailments, understand how you built your cage, how you got there/ It's not my job, everyone has their own story, and you have to rework it on your own with self-analysis or better yet, assisted by a therapist who can speed up the analysis process. I recommend cognitive behavioral therapy known as CBT. Not all psychologists are the same, each of them is different. So in finding the right professional I will make your task easier. Look for those who do this therapy, because in a few words they will help you rewrite in your mind a different story from how it is written now. I use simple words which are very helpful. Another piece of advice I give you is to attend him for at least six months. Give yourself this time horizon. Better if a year. Often going to the psychologist in the imagination of many people is something profoundly negative which in some cases is the result of conventional legacies of society that generate the famous feeling of shame. I told you about it. The association that is still made with regard to mental care is very often of the type: - "you go to the psychologist so you're crazy.."- or other amenities. In the year of our Lord 2024, it seems impossible, but there are still those who make these arguments. On the basis of these limiting beliefs, many experience the approach to the professional very badly, and generally after a few sessions they run away and never show up again. Let's see if I can overwrite this incorrectly perceived concept. If you have a cavity and don't treat it, then you lose the tooth, right? What is the difference between dental care and mental care? None. If you have a 70 euro teeth cleaning every year you reduce the risk of spending a fortune on a dental implant that costs at least 1500. How many cleanings do you get with 1500 euros? At least 20, so in twenty years you're good, or you're toothless because you don't have all that money in one lump sum, is it true or not? It's the same thing with the mind, it gets 'dirty' like teeth. Except that what stains and damages it is not the drinks or sugar but the negative emotions, the unsaid or swallowed toads, the micro traumas or macro traumas left there. The ignored anxieties, the too many "I don't have time" or "now is not the time" Often the experience with someone who is not specialized in the field that interests us reinforces this belief. If you need fruit and go to the butcher, what can he do for you? If you want to learn to dance ballet and instead you go to an aerobics instructor, whose fault is it? Having said that, do whatever you want. Know that, if you turn to a therapist as I recommend, you must make sure that he or she is familiar with CBT. Do research on the internet, look at several, then choose. But the field where you have to look is this. Let's go back to the cage. Don't confuse it with the so-called "comfort zone", it has nothing to do with it but it is easy to confuse the concepts. Where you are is a cage that generates discomfort that you are not aware of or, if you are, it is a place from which you cannot escape on your own. Then Panic arrives, but he can't open the door, he can only shake it, bang on the bars etc. If he terrifies you it's to get you out of there. I'm sure this is clear by now. What could happen though? It could happen that the people around you who love you tend to form a circle around you, keeping you overly protected, treating you almost like a child to be protected. This should be absolutely avoided because it could introduce you to other members of the large Panico family. You already know anxiety and stress, let's leave exhaustion and depression where they are, but the family is large. You may know agoraphobia, claustrophobia, hypochondriasis...phobia. Phobias are films that your mind projects onto a screen located in your mind, in the visual cortex. They give macabre shows at all hours, do you want to go to this kind of cinema? Do you understand why I want you to go out with me to go find Panico and chase him?

I'm not saying it's easy, especially if you're new to it. And I, my darling, know well what I'm talking about. You already know part of my story. After I quit as a truck driver I was convinced that I would never drive a car again. I had started watching movies in my mind. I had waited so long to address the issue that not only did I have panic attacks while driving the company vehicle, but also while I was driving mine. And what did my family do? Don't worry, we'll drive. And I was a passenger...for about a month. I felt part of a disability that profoundly humiliated me on the one hand but that I didn't know how to resolve on the other. Then my combative nature awoke after Panic had come knocking forcefully on my cage for the umpteenth time. So I started getting into the car, feeling Anxiety next to me and driving alone for kilometers and kilometers. When it was too much I stopped and then started again. But with immense effort I had managed to dissociate driving from fear. Not totally. And not right away. I've looked for the magic wand a thousand times but I still haven't found it. That was a first step, getting back on the horse. Meanwhile. A step at a time. I was out of the cage, standing in the doorway, and I knew where to look for him. At a specific point on the highway. So I trained for the fateful moment, I didn't need anticipatory anxiety, I knew exactly where to go to play the tennis match that we know. And so one day I left. And he was there, waiting for me. I no longer started from a score of 10 to 1, I was already 7 to 4. I was loaded like a mine. I chose Sunday to make the trip, there are no trucks, the motorway is free during the year and I could go as slowly as I wanted, always in safety of course. I get ready I do my reverse breathing for five minutes before leaving and off I go. At the exit where it all began, here he comes, I start to breathe through one nostril, I slow down and move forward, he presses hard.. now at less than 60 per hour I see the lay-by and I even turn on the indicator, I didn't have any cars nearby, I could have done it but I resisted by continuing to breathe through one nostril... a couple of kilometers like that and it disappeared completely. I was very happy, it wasn't a victory but at least I hadn't lost badly. The return journey was a marvel. I hadn't solved it yet, but I had rewritten in my mind an epilogue that I took for granted. Until a week before, it had been impossible to do that thing again and instead I had done it. It may seem absurd to you but every time I drive long distances today, I am grateful for every journey. Something that was taken for granted until 2021, such as driving and moving, at a certain point was no longer so, it had been taken away from me, they had deprived me of the joy of driving. There I learned to take nothing for granted and to be grateful. I am grateful to Panico because now I appreciate something that I previously took for granted, and apparently nothing in life is taken for granted. We realize the importance of things when we lose them. It is what is called a cliché, but applied to this case it becomes full of meaning. What would have happened if I had accepted the help and support of my family who, thinking they were doing me good, were doing me harm? Now I wouldn't drive anywhere again. If I had remained in the cage, if I had simply escaped from that situation I would have solved the discomfort but I would have lived without something. I wasn't willing to give up that something. I don't know if it will happen again, I don't even think about it happening again, if it were I already know what to do, my racket is always ready. It is an immense personal satisfaction that you cannot deprive yourself of. It's what they call a "win experience". There are games in life that you can choose not to play and others that you have to face. Do you remember Elisa's case? What should he have done? No longer going to work, staying locked up at home for life? Certainly she did it like this for the first three months, then for six months she was always accompanied by her father who didn't leave her alone, then she started moving alone, also stopping herself driving for fear of being followed, today she pays extreme attention to everyone those who ring the doorbell of the shop especially if she has never seen them but she is there, she has left again. It takes time. Diego also continues to work, and if it happens again he will do his exercises again... patience and perseverance love, patience and perseverance.

This is why I want you to go out, I'm not telling you to go out immediately and go to the place that causes you discomfort or to the situation that seems impossible to deal with. I want you to train with those two simple breathing techniques, I could have put ten, I put two, if you don't like them search on the web, maybe you'll find a better technique or one more suitable for you. But this is the first step. Start preparing, start equipping yourself with the tools that will allow you to go and play the game, and replay it again and again and again. There will be many games darling, and I want you to always have your tools of the trade. Panico is there because you need it. You don't have to be afraid of it. See what he wants. But please, I beg you, open that cage my love. Stand at the entrance. A step at a time. Now let's look at other cases that are perhaps similar to yours. But first let's also look at those visualization techniques I was telling you about. One last recommendation. Everything you have to do, you have to do yourself.

Nobody can do it for you. A therapist can help you to rework, as we said, family members can help you in the early days but then there is you and only you. Panic came from you not from others. It's you who has to do the math. Absolutely avoid the so-called "phobic partner". That is, a fixed person or several people who assist you in the things you do. Especially if they are people who reveal their concern perhaps while you are in the eye of the storm face to face with a Panic visit. Avoid. And also avoid talking about it with everyone all the time. The more you talk about a problem or something you consider as such, the more it becomes stronger, the more you press the same button and the more you fix the frequency of referrals. An effective technique is to talk about it as little as possible once you have taken stock of the situation. The objective is to take away its strength, to change the relationship of incidence and impact. Deflate, resize, train. Take this opportunity to understand how to improve your life. You are not the first and you will not be the last. After two years I met him again, he asked me to play a quick game and I won in ten minutes. But I also looked up and I seem to recognize some bars, without realizing I was rebuilding the cage. The dismissal, the employment center, the CVs to send... and like in 2021... it's like... it's not 2021, I'm in 2024, but this is to make you understand how strong it can be stimulation by association. Without thinking, I pressed the keys associated with a period linked to Panic and my mind recalled it. Even without Anxiety and Stress, he showed up automatically, no longer in the car but at home... do you know what the difference is between today and three years ago?

My preparation, the racket always ready, the elaboration, the self-analysis that revealed the similarities responsible for the erroneous response that my mind generated... it's as if, but it's not.

So let's see something about visualization? Do you want? Take a break maybe, because it's a little more demanding. But on the other hand you will shift the focus to something new. This helps too. Everything you know more is an extra racket to use when needed if needed. It's your time, it's time to dedicate yourself to you, to you and no one else I repeat.

Chapter 7

"The visualization"

Visualization is a technique that I define as complex, but in itself it is not the most suitable term. Let's say it requires some energy to concentrate. First of all you have to close your eyes and then imagine. Here too, there are myriads of techniques and myriads of images to think about. But you must be wondering what to think, what to imagine, right?
And you have a good reason for it. The purpose of this technique is to create a positive image in the mind that gives us a sense of tranquility and protection. Visualization is also used in personal growth courses to attract those specific

circumstances/frequencies. Here opens the door that leads to the now well-known quantum physics and the law of attraction of which you will find myriads of notions and manuscripts, so I will gloss over, if you allow me, the topic, also because I call it the law of abstraction and not of attraction so I am not the best person to tell you about it. Practice in learning to visualize becomes fundamental. How can you get started? And what do you need to visualize then? Start with geometric shapes. Close your eyes and imagine a circle, or a square, or a triangle. Whatever you want. Then elaborate your vision, if you have imagined a circle, now force yourself to imagine a sphere, if you have imagined a square now imagine a cube, if you have imagined a triangle visualize a pyramid or a cone. Think of the ice cream cone it's even easier. Repeat these exercises until you are able to fix each image in your mind for more than ten seconds. This is training, we don't need it for our purpose. We need it to become familiar with this visual faculty of your mind, to activate it and make it usable. It's like loading a new application on your phone. You have to download. Well.

Once it becomes natural and effortless for you to fix images you can move on to the next phase. The Upgrade. You have learned to visualize, now you must apply this new ability of yours to use it to give you benefits, relaxation and a sense of calm and protection. Who or what would you like by your side in difficult and fearful moments? A bodyguard? An animal? An angel? A dragon? A unicorn? A phoenix? A gnome? A fair? An elf? A sword? A shield? A symbol? Think, imagine reflect. What does the sense of protection represent in your heart. What is protection for you, how would you represent it? This is totally subjective here. I've given some ideas but the possibilities are endless. So before you continue reading, I ask you to stop and think about it a bit, take your time, my book will have less than a hundred pages so you have plenty of time to go ahead and finish it. Or at least bookmark this part of the techniques because you will have to train to learn how to use them and it will take a while. Like when you learned to ride a bicycle without training wheels, do you remember that?

I give you another suggestion to speed up the practice of this learning. At the beginning I was struggling a lot. I couldn't hold an image for more than a couple of seconds. I kept changing things to imagine. Then I tried to change strategy. I took pen and paper and drew. For geometric shapes everything is fine, for freehand drawings of animals or angels however, despite having tried to try my hand several times there was nothing to do, I am totally denied for drawing. So I went to Google, looked for images, printed them out, then started the exercise. Look at the drawn or printed image. Observe the colors, the depth, fixate on one point. Then change where you are staring, then close your eyes and recall what you just saw. This technique greatly increases your capacity. It is immediate and direct. It makes everything easier. I remember that I had no papers at home. I hadn't been to school for a while now. So I bought a ream of paper at the stationery shop, for two euros I had plenty, then I also bought a pack of pencil colours. So even if I'm not good at having them there in my free time, I confess that I found benefit from the drawing activity. For me it was a pleasant discovery. Extremely relaxing. A cheap hobby. I suggest you try it.

Now this technique that I expect you to have learned helps you both in the phases of anticipatory anxiety and in moments of conversation with panic. But you can also use it for no reason simply to relax. It only takes a few seconds. Especially if you're feeling a little down. A few seconds, you visualize your guardian in the form or appearance that you have decided and as if by magic your frequencies rise, and the body will be flooded with endorphins, feel-good hormones. They don't sell these commercially, you have to produce them yourself. According to some, a little chocolate helps. But it's always your mind that gives the input. This is also a key, and the frequency and associated tone are positive. The note that chocolate gives you is the association of the party with joy, perhaps with the reunited family, all pleasant sensations experienced in childhood which have overwritten sensations of happiness and crazy joy in the mind, because they are generally fixed by very strong and intense emotions which only you can try them as children. However, if you did not have a happy childhood as they say, if you are among those souls who had to experience pain in that phase of life for whatever reason, then I and all the members of the "panic club" are ideally to your aid. I want you to feel our embrace and our warmth around you. And I want all those who had a happy childhood to direct a thought of love towards those children of today and yesterday who did not have this privilege. I want you now that you have learned visualization, to imagine sending a package containing a heart of light to these people you don't even know. Then I also want you to think of gratitude for the good moments you have had and will have. What I'm asking you reminds me of something else. It has nothing to do with visualization, but it has something to do with frequencies and the stimulation of inner well-being. It's called "ho'oponopono" a rather bizarre name, which is endearing. Maybe you already know it. "Ho'ponopono" is a mantra. The power of mantras lies in what they call the strength of words, because even words, their pronunciation in particular, seem to generate positive frequencies, positive vibrations. I believe that emotional associations have something to do with this too. However, this mantra is made up of four words to be pronounced repeatedly for a few minutes. The words are these: -"I'm sorry, Forgive me, I love you, Thank you". Simple, right? Well.

I tell you that for your personal pleasure you can associate the positive stimuli of visualization with the vocal ones that stimulate the sense of hearing. Do you remember that in breathing we associated the mental effort to control the breathing with the sense of touch with the touch of the nostril or belly? Well. Here we always use a mental faculty, imagination, and we add another of the five senses. Hearing. I still do it today when I have some free time to recharge my good mood batteries.

Imagine a star. Now stand up, spread your legs a little wider than shoulder width and extend your arms parallel to the ground laterally. It's complicated? You have to make the shape of the star with your body, arms and legs wide open to the sides. Have you ever seen Leonardo Da Vinci's Vitruvian Man? If so, be like him. If you've never seen him, go to Google and write "Vitruvian man". You are here? Well.

You are now a star. This star has 5 vertices, the head, arms and legs. Now starting from your left arm, associate a word and say it out loud. Then associate another one with the head, then one for the right hand, one for the right leg and finally one for the left leg. Concentrate again. And create your own mantra associated with the star you have become. You're a star.

This is a very complex technique, only apparently easy, but which offers enormous benefits. I share with you the mantra that I associated with this exercise taught to me in a personal growth course. It helps increase self-esteem. You can change the words as you want.

HEALTH

MONEY
SUCCESS

POWER
PROTECTION

Funny right? Motivating? Yes. So let's see another example that involves your 'self' like physical and mental gymnastics, let's see the triangle.
Now keep your legs apart a little wider than your shoulders and join your arms upwards, joining the palms of your hands. The arms go up and touch the palms. You are now a triangle. You concentrate on the vertex where your hands are and pronounce out loud -"Light" then you concentrate on the right leg and pronounce -"Victory" then you concentrate on the left leg and pronounce the word -"Love' '.
Repeat these exercises for 5 minutes a day.
Remember that you are training to go after Panico and face him in several tennis matches. Train. He gets stronger. You don't know how many more games you'll have to play, no one knows, so when in doubt, always be in top form.

LIGHT

Well. However, the chapter is not over yet. I hope
the digression was of interest and enjoyment to you.
A nice and curious variation on the theme, a bit of
gymnastics, even if static, is always good.
The visualization includes one last exercise, and the
introduction of another figure that the therapists are
familiar with. I'm talking about the "Daimon", a sort
of guardian who comes out of the religious vision
that maybe you, like me, have, and refers to the
angels usually depicted in iconography with human
features, and enters a more secular dimension that
sees this guardian in different forms, including
animals. Visualizing this being, this entity,
imagining having it next to us now, should be very
simple for you. Close your eyes and imagine
yourself with this luminous being at your side, it

must shed light like a lamp in the shape of a cat or rabbit or dragon or lion. Help yourself by also thinking about the "Patronus" from the "Harry Potter" saga. If you haven't seen it, always go to Google and write "patronus harry potter" and you will understand what I'm talking about and it will help you find the image to reproduce in your mind. I know that I ask a lot of you, I know that I urge you and invite you to action from time to time. But if you want something you have to move. I also moved, I also did research. All in all you have half a job ready to train and overcome Panic. As I already told you, you have to do the other half of the work. He came to you, he wants to play and be chased to get you away from the cage where you have decided to hole up. Well.

The work on you is important. It is important that you increase your self-esteem. It is important that you begin to conceive in your mind the progress, the victory, the light at the end of the tunnel, the overcoming of the unresolved issue or issues that have put you face to face with Mr. Panic's attacks. That's what we're here for, right? Well.

As it stands he is stronger than you, he pushes you down a hill and you can't stop him. You are on this book, on this road, to pull the handbrake and reverse the roles, you have to get to the point of being the one chasing him. It's you who pushes him away, it's you who wins tennis matches with him. And before now you weren't trained to do it.

Now whenever you feel any unpleasant sensation, visualize yourself with this light next to you. You need this so you don't feel alone. There is someone with you, there are two of you. And he is alone. So it is very likely that at the unpleasant sensation that precedes it, he decides to stop and not disturb you. This is the meaning.

Now the score is 6 to 5 for him. You're close to equalizing and taking the lead. Stay here, train, I want you to want to meet him to see your progress. Is absurd? No, it's the paradigm that we overturned together. You have to be eager for the next match with Panico to see how much strength he has lost. But above all how much have you earned.

After my first encounters with him, I had learned, and perhaps you have learned too, to sense his arrival a few minutes before he started making noise in my space. This happens when you learn to be centered. It's a good sign. Depriving Panic of the surprise effect represents a big advantage. But we must not delude ourselves, as I did, that this is enough. It's a nice advantage not to be caught unprepared, right? But it's not enough, we have to stop him from coming any closer. In order to achieve this result, as mentioned, you need to move away from the cage.

Well now let's continue talking about techniques to use during our friend's visits. The next technique involves always involving touch, in a more energetic and decisive way in addition to the use of the voice. And I could call it shock therapy. It is useful to all those who are in the primordial phase of the soap opera. That is, all those who have only had very few encounters with Panic, between one and three times. In theory you haven't measured him out yet if you've only met him for a short time. As is the case for many, the most intense phases that generate future fears concern the abrupt ways in which Panic shakes us. Sensation of tightness in the chest which leads the mind to fear that there is a heart attack in progress, shortness of breath, tachycardia, tremor in the legs, spasms and for some stiffening similar to paralysis of one or more parts of the body, all accompanied by a mixed perception to belief of imminent death. Now we know that he enters our head and preaches, as mentioned, but if we speak with internal dialogue or mantras he remains silent. Physical sensations remain to be contained. Our mind is tricked by stimuli that send the wrong signals. They are associations. Pressure on the chest = heart attack. But it's a feeling, it's not real. How do we block it? I pressed all five fingertips firmly against my chest. This generated real physical pressure. And then I released, generating physical decompression. I repeated this movement, these pressures at least ten times. What is this energetic technique for? To make the mind understand that the only real pressure is the one I exert myself, as if to say, I am the one who compresses. Furthermore, decompression helps the sensation of relaxation, because by releasing the sternum you feel a relaxation, certainly induced, but still a relaxation, a decompression, an artificial distension. Then open your hand, lightly close your fingertips and push firmly into your chest. You have to press, don't hit the chest please. And then take your hand away, repeat this exercise. Pressure relief, pressure relief. Well.

Another alternative is to exert firm pressure with the index finger and thumb on the sides of the nail of the other thumb, almost creating a pincer effect, also in this case applying pressure during the peak. Press and release, press and release. The last variable of this type concerns the use of small pinches on the back of the hand. You have to give them as if you were squeezing the air bubbles of the bubble wrap used to make packaging. Associated with this technique, the phrase must be pronounced mentally or verbally: -"it's ok, I'm here. It's ok I'm here, it's ok, it's ok, it's ok". These very energetic techniques must be applied in the first episodes, here too, choose one of the three. Apply this until you automatically do both the physical touch part and the phrase repetition that involves repeating each of the two statements three times.

All of this is to mentally prepare you for unexpected visits. Once you have chosen and assimilated a technique you will gradually reduce the impact of events. It is understood that if you do not identify the trigger that calls Panic near you and your space, he will continue to stay. He cannot be fooled, for him getting you out of the cage is the mission. Evidently if he chose you it's because you deserve to be helped. Your life is not good.

You absolutely must acquire this awareness. You don't have a problem, you have a solution. Something inside you has called upon superior forces created to save the deserving, you are the wild animal entangled in a net, they are trying to free you. There's no need to just resist. Confronting this gentleman who is still someone on your side is only the first step. Then when you are free you have to understand how to avoid twisting your life around something harmful to you. Accepting situations is a good viaticum for serenity. Acknowledging that superficial and conscious acceptance is not enough is the last call to change things. In my experience there were many things that I considered positive that led me to fight to stay doing what I was doing, but after two years of back and forth I reached my breaking point. And I changed. It wasn't easy, but if I hadn't done it at that moment I wouldn't be where I am now. Five days have passed since the revival with Panico. I'm wonderful. I processed it as a visit from an old friend who came to see how I was and if I was still training.

If you read other manuals, or other articles on the subject, you will find techniques as an end in themselves without practical application, explained by professors who clearly don't know what they're talking about. The vision I provide you is first of all diametrically opposed to any other theory. I'm not telling you that you have a problem, or a pathology. I tell you that you have a solution, an opportunity. I tell you that it comes from two causes, traumatic event caused by external agents, or accumulation of excess anxiety and stress in the emotional tank. I'll tell you which psychologist to go to and not in general. I provide you with the tools to deal with it immediately and in the long term. Another thing that you might find but which I advise you not to follow are handbooks, lists which according to some are useful for prevention. These lists that are good in every season on anything are for example: don't take caffeine, don't smoke, use dim lights, don't use bright colors that could excite and agitate you (yes, you understood correctly, you have panic attacks because maybe you're wearing clothes with colors that are too bright...I swear I found this nonsense too). Why do I advise you against them? Because they are mechanisms that you would implement, entrenching your condition as a victim, as prey, and on an unconscious level you would carry out an intensive cultivation of anticipatory anxiety. You don't have to run away in panic, you have to do exactly the opposite. As I taught you. Understand it, understand it, acknowledge that it is there to help you. Then you have to do a self-analysis, either alone or better with a specific professional. Since you don't solve it right away, I also give you some tools to face it, to defeat it, to chase it, to reduce the balance of power. From the series:

-" Ok Mr Panico, you've come by, I thank you for letting me know that I'm ill, I hadn't noticed on my own, but now thanks for your visit, from here on out, I'll lead my life. Come back anytime so I can show you my progress. Bye bye"-

It's very different, it's an absolutely innovative perspective. What changes is your attitude. This will give you enormous strength that will serve you and change your life. Once such a blow has passed, in an average time of two to three years nothing will scare you anymore. You will face anything with medals on your chest. They will look at you like an alien when you are calm while everyone else is agitated. You will shed light my darling. In the next chapter we will see other testimonies. We will need them to understand that Panic starts from very far away when he arrives in our lives. Before he comes to visit us he goes on a long journey, except of course in cases where he shows up immediately after an accidental trauma that you cannot act on.

Chapter 8

"More stories, you're in good company"

Yep, you're in good company. You thought it only happened to you, but instead at least one in ten people you meet know about Panico, either in person or through friends and family. It's just you who faces it, it's you who has to play the game, let's be clear, but knowing that others like you are playing the same game on other fields is already different.
Let's start with Franco's story. Franco meets Panico one day for lunch at his house. In front of his mother and father, who at times has a real heart attack seeing their only son at the mercy of Panic's tugs, it's the first time and they don't understand what's happening. They call 118, the doctors arrive and fortunately after routine checks at home, measuring blood pressure, asking questions, they understand that it was a panic attack. From when Franco is at the table and begins to tremble, putting a hand on his chest with his legs shaking and banging on the legs of the table, about twenty minutes pass by the time the 118 doctors arrive, so Panico was already almost tired of pulling the poor man. Franco was treacherously struck like all of us the first time.

Franco's research started from there, he only had four or five meetings with the therapist then he talked a lot with a friend of his who had already known Panico for a year, and in the acute phases which lasted a year he used anxiolytics prescribed by general practitioner, who obviously prevented the occurrence of his encounters and attenuated them. Then by chance we meet in a work context. I immediately understood that he hadn't understood anything. He thought he could solve it with drugs, he had branded the psychologist he had only been seeing for a month as someone who didn't understand anything and had deluded himself that thanks to the prescriptions of his GP he would be able to live with it. I immediately explained to him that anxiolytics are for anxiety, not for panic. Because Ansia comes to visit you and stays close to you more or less during most of the day for a more or less long period, Panico on the other hand is more of a type who blitz, enters, strikes and exits. I used the colander metaphor. I told him that he was trying to collect water with a colander. The water was Panic to be stopped or harnessed, the colander was the anxiolytics. I won't dwell on this because I have already explained these things to you, and you remember them right?. Well.

I remember him looking at me almost shocked. And he didn't speak. And I, who know a little about communication, didn't speak. I didn't offer to give

him any suggestions because they hadn't been asked of me. Instead, after several seconds, in which he probably visualized the water coming out of the colander, he said to me:-"so what the fuck should I do, eh?"-He did it with a certain frown, and with a very bothersome. With the attitude of someone who is in the phase in which he has understood that he is doing something wrong but he is afraid to admit it, especially to a stranger. He immediately added: "Are you a doctor who talks so much?"
I burst out laughing without taking up the provocation, it was his way of asking me for help, and the challenging, almost exasperated tone was the answer to the problem. Another would have sent him to hell, not me. Because I understood. I replied to him like this: -"I'm not a doctor, but I know a good one who assists you in the self-analysis process, it's a kind of coupon that must be done combined with other things, I got out of it in one year after two years I lived with it, also learning to anticipate and block it, but in the end I had to give in and close the accounts to get rid of the thought." At that point his attitude changed radically towards me, his body language was no longer hostile. Do you know why? Because she had just identified me as similar to her. We had something in common, a mutual friend, so he opened up and told me that it always happened to him at lunch, five or six times a month. I immediately asked what generated anxiety and

stress because that's where we start. He replied that he had broken up with his girlfriend with whom he had been with for ten years. Her decision wasn't his, but hers, and he couldn't accept it. She had made big plans in her head and couldn't understand why she didn't want to be with him anymore. I explained to him that in couple relationships it is not written anywhere that there must be a reason for separation. We must accept that at any moment the partner may decide to break away just because she feels she has to. For no reason. The source of his unease arose not so much from the end of the story itself, but from the fact of not having a logical explanation, he had started to mull over this. He had fixed thoughts which basically led him to develop imaginary theories which however produced real negative emotions. This intense psychic activity had begun to fill his emotional tank with sludge. Based on this intuition of mine, I suggested that he turn to a therapist and rework the end of the story in order to accept it and move forward.

He asked me why I thought they happened at lunch. I replied that there were two cases. A random one, that is, the emotional tank overflowed while he was at the table and since you can't choose the place of the meeting it was simply like that. The second hypothesis, which however required a more in-depth investigation, was to be linked to food. But how? I asked if by any chance he had ever had problems with eating disorders and he replied no, but he told me that in the ten years together, the two worked in a restaurant, he in the kitchen and she at the tables serving. Here's the connection with food. By some strange mental association he had linked the dishes to the discomfort associated with the person. That was the fuse that triggered the explosion. This testimony makes us understand how complex unconscious mental associations sometimes are. I had had an excellent intuition but at that point he had to do the work on himself together with the therapist. We lost touch with each other for a few months, when I saw him again he said that progressively with the re-elaboration and self-analysis combined with the change of profession, Panico had fled and had no longer had any visitors. He had moved away from the cage. The bars were the constant negative thoughts represented by the hypotheses he made about the end of the story based on nothing but which, as mentioned, generated the frequencies of Anxiety and Stress. He hurt himself in a nutshell. The recurring thought was that of her entwined with another, a faceless body that according to him and only according to him, was responsible for the end of her story, another man who satisfied her was the thought of her that sent him into a tailspin. He used negative visualization. The effects were the same as positive visualization. Instead of mentally creating the image of a Daimon that emanated light and protected him, he had created a monster that he constantly fed. Who knows how far he would have come to imagine. These situations can happen to anyone and unfortunately certain self-generated worms lead in the long run to the commission of reckless acts. Luckily for Franco, Panico arrived to save him before it was too late. First, for example, that persecutory delusions took possession of his mind. So he too understood that he had to be grateful for what had happened to him. The next testimony is that of Lucia. Lucia works as a waitress, she studied at the hotel institute and she likes her job very much. She is the second born of three siblings. You specify the degree of kinship because I have discovered that the psychological and character profile of many individuals is strongly connected to family status. Only children tend to resemble each other in behavior, first-borns ditto and consequently also middle-aged and youngest children. Now, one of the characteristics common to middle children is that they tend to want to demonstrate and do a lot to attract attention, they always have a great need for consideration and gratification otherwise they live badly. Why does this dynamic happen in most of them? Because intimately it is possible that in childhood and adolescence they felt less considered than the eldest and youngest. In a simplistic way I could summarize this complicated dynamic as follows: the first-born attracts the parents' attention because he is the first to do anything for his parents, the last-born attracts their parents' attention because instinctively he is the one who requires the most care and protection . Not out of malice, therefore, but for these reasons, parents tend to unbalance attention and consideration to the detriment of the pimp. It is not an absolute rule, but it concerns many individuals. So the need to attract the attention and love of parents to claim their own dose of love is created in a person's head. What happens after adolescence? In adulthood, those with this profile will tend to project the dynamics implemented towards the parental figure onto other people, generally a teacher, a doctor, a boss, etc.

They are people who essentially always try to stand out and seek approval, compliments and rewards. When this doesn't happen, the world comes crashing down on them and so they increase their work to get noticed, come into conflict with other colleagues, and can even end up falling prey to phenomena of victimization. Lucia does not differ from this description. For her, doing everything well and possibly before others and having it noticed by the owner is a source of pride, becoming the owner's trusted person represents an immense joy. For a while Lucia manages to have a lot of satisfaction even if she is sometimes literally exploited. But she doesn't mind being exploited, she cares that she is told she is good and that she is entrusted with responsibilities such as managing the cash register that other colleagues are not granted. This makes her feel loved, respected and considered and even if she returns home exhausted from work, having received the compliment from the owner and her clients literally makes her enthusiasm skyrocket. She finds it difficult to fall asleep due to the adrenaline given by the joy on certain evenings. So everything goes well, until when?... until someone else arrives and draws the owner's attention to himself, thus taking it away from Lucia. These subjects immediately enter into competition, immediately put their rival in their sights and prepare for war in no time. In love relationships they tend to be particularly jealous. I open parentheses, what I am talking about once again are ways of being, I refrain from making judgments or establishing right, wrong, good and evil. I have already said that these evaluations do not exist in my reality. There are only ways of being and everyone has their own. Closed parenthesis.

Let's go back to Lucia's story. Her family had a bad relationship with her brothers who always seemed more deserving of parental attention than her, she went out of her way even at home in the illusion that her mother or father would say thank you for her . It's not that her parents were bad or that they loved her less than her siblings, it's simply that when one doesn't cause problems and takes the work out of your hands, you take it for granted and cancel out any form of concern towards her by directing your energies towards those gives them problems. So going to work and finding what she couldn't find at home represented her balance for her, just like a scale. On one plate the negative weight of a family that didn't give her the right consideration and on the other a job that gave her satisfaction to the extent she desired. The balance, however, when you delegate your serenity and happiness to external agents is precarious, in fact if these change your emotional state also changes. Right? Well.

One fine day Lucia's owner shows up at work with a new partner. For Lucia it's not a problem, she's had other women and her owner doesn't care about her love, it's not what she's looking for. She thrives on the rewards and responsibilities he entrusts to her. Except that, unlike the others, this woman begins to frequent the work environment a lot, she talks to customers, gives a hand in matters and therefore begins to occupy a space that was previously covered from Lucia. But the situation still does not trigger reactions on Lucia. She's still the favorite at work. Until one day the owner calls together his team and announces that Maria, his partner, will start working permanently at the restaurant. Her duties will be in the dining room taking orders and later at the cash register. Open heaven! Very dark clouds begin to gather in Lucia's head on the horizon. It's why on earth you're wondering. Have you had a demotion? Will she get less money? No. So what triggers the fatal wrath? She should be happy to have some sort of relief from homework. Yet even though she would have worked a little less for the same money, she has a very bad experience with the new entry. She experiences the decline in attention towards her by the owner at work. She feels devalued. The world literally falls on her. In her head she begins to resent Maria. She talks about it behind her back to her other colleagues, as soon as she makes the slightest mistake she immediately points it out to her boss and her colleagues, she starts trying to belittle and destroy what she considered to be an intruder. Her boss was seen as her personal distributor of well-being in the form of special tasks and compliments and now that distributor no longer gives out a reward even if you pay gold for it. He is always around her at work, he smiles at her, he hugs her, he is close to her when customers arrive at the checkout. Lucia also tries in other ways to win back the attentions of her owner for the reasons we have said but she feels she can no longer compete with his new flame. So she starts to feel bad at work, she is nervous because she is physically tired and there is no longer any adrenaline to keep her going. She returns home nervous and tries to take out her anger and frustration on her brothers and parents too. In other words, she starts throwing tantrums to get someone's attention. After a few months like this, in your opinion, what had Lucia filled her emotional tank with? Of anger, nervousness and stress. Exact. Soon this mix of negative emotions generated a nice distillation of anxiety. She began to feel nervous before going to work. The work was always the same, she worked even less. The same place, the same salary. Yet his perception of her was distorted. Instead of changing jobs, however, she continued to get hurt. She would find work wherever she asked. But nothing persisted in staying there and ignoring Ansia's good-natured warnings. The day also came when Anxiety, now fed up with being ignored, called Panic. And he arrived. In the dining room, in front of an entire table of customers, her legs shaking, her breathing labored, the tears falling from her eyes and then down to the ground, fortunately without slamming violently, simply going down because her legs couldn't hold up. A true "patatrac" in style. However, something happens there which, if possible, worsens the situation. Its owner, Filiberto arrives, called by one of the customers and by the loud shouting that had arisen in the room with many people including a doctor, who had approached to provide help and assistance, and sees her on the ground with a conclave of people around. He kneels down, talks to the doctor and appears very worried about her. That spontaneous and natural attitude unconsciously feeds Lucia again with the hope of regaining the consideration she was looking for, the wellness distributor had started to unload nourishment for her mind again.

Yes, you understood correctly, she was happy again, for Panico's visit but not for the right reasons, evidently. Panic had arrived to tell her:

-"get out of this place, try to understand that you are important regardless of the consideration of an owner. Process this need of yours, you deserve to be happy, why do you persist in staying here? Why don't you understand that your mind has created a reality distorted by incorrect emotional perceptions that makes you feel bad? You didn't come into the world to feel bad" -

Needless to say, she didn't even remotely think about all these exhortations from Panic. She associated feeling ill with the arrival of the owner who suddenly had all the attention in the world for her. This is very dangerous, but it can happen in subjects predisposed to experiencing these dynamics. Ergo. If discomfort becomes a vehicle to obtain the consideration I crave, then discomfort, panic attacks and other trumps are welcome. The evolution of this attitude which I could define as 'love wanted' can lead to hypochondria. As you may have understood, Lucia continued to go to work and once a week she played a tennis match in the living room. Now not only her boss, but all her colleagues and even some regular customers had their eyes only for her. Panico was not at all happy with the situation. He hadn't come to her to make her live in constant pity. It was pleasant for her, after so many years, all that attention from all those people was a bit like winning the lottery. But our friend had a mission, to restore Lucia's inner balance. As it was for me, she began to cause disabling physical blockages, for me it was gastritis as I told you, for her it was a blocked back. Completely blocked. To the point of preventing her from going to work. Does this seem incredible to you? Yet that's how she went. In the end, also thanks to her meeting with a loving boy, Lucia left her job and threw herself into another professional field. She didn't need a therapist, drugs or self-analysis. Let's say that you have a very active guardian angel. What considerations did I feel like making when analyzing this case? That sometimes nothing is needed. This is also a success story. Based on logic, however, I can predict that should her love disappear from her life, her panic will await her. I preach awareness and self-analysis as you well know, I even urge you to turn to a therapist because I believe I have understood well who Panico is and why he intervenes as an ally in our lives. But I also have the open-mindedness to admit that sometimes other random factors simply intervene in life that divert the course of events and keep us afloat. After all, it is not written anywhere that a person necessarily has to evolve their level of awareness and they are fine without it. Lucia's is undoubtedly the case that best represents this case. I wanted to share this story with you even though I could have omitted it and told you that you have to follow my advice. But that's not my style. I'm just here to make you understand that you don't have a problem but an opportunity, and that a lot of people come out of it. This in my intent, wants to change your approach to the situation you are experiencing as consequences of other facts that Panico tries to bring to your attention. The next story is very similar to Lucia's but has an epilogue, or rather a slightly different development. The protagonist this time is a boy, Edoardo.

Edoardo is a barman, he also comes from hotel school, he too has been experiencing a conflictual relationship in his family for years. He is the second born of two children, the youngest. When Edo is in his penultimate year of high school his sister Marzia graduates. She is a rebel and during her adolescence she did more than the devil did. Her extreme behavior generated tension and great embarrassment at home. She even went so far as to report her parents for mistreatment as a form of retaliation for a sort of denied authorization. I'll spare you the details because she isn't the protagonist here but only represents a trigger. Following her complaint, a forty-eight happened. Social workers, psychologists, trials... in short, a difficult situation. In the middle of the fight between Marzia and her parents there was Edo, who studied and worked trying not to absorb the negative energies that had been hovering in the house for months. The epilogue of the issue between the sister and her parents occurred after about a year, with the sister kicked out of the house by her parents. For more than a year no one knew anything about Marzia. Her parents felt betrayed to the point that they no longer wanted to look for her, they experienced that very serious situation almost as a relief. This event represented a real trauma for Edoardo. He got it into his head that his parents would throw him out of the house too, and so he started living his life as a teenager trying in every way to please his parents in everything. He even paid the groceries and bills at a time of financial difficulty for his parents. The situation at home was heavy and Edoardo's mother had accumulated a great deal of anger over the years. This anger made her intractable. It was due to a hidden form of guilt. Edo's mother felt guilty for the daughter she no longer knew anything about, she felt guilty for the failure of the clothing store she ran with her husband and tuned into this frequency she also became aggressive towards her son, even though the latter was went out of his way to help, becoming the only source of income in the house at just eighteen years old. Edoardo's father had fallen into depression, his love for his wife prevented him from curbing his behavior and seeing his son working to pay for his groceries was a very heavy blow to his ego as a man.

Then he wobbled and fell into depression. Edoardo was unknowingly filling his emotional tank with fear, guilt, anxiety and stress. In short, the usual cocktail. Except that one day, he receives a job offer in a hotel one hundred kilometers from home, in the Alps. Given the certainly interesting financial offer, he decides to accept it. When he communicates this at home, his mother goes into a rage, and to cut a long story short, she makes him understand, almost threatening him, that even if he leaves home he will have to continue sending money to repay all the money she had spent on him since when he was a child. Think about it? I think it's one of the worst things a parent can say to you. Everyone is made in their own way, everyone has the same sensitivity as him, I would have reacted by sending her to hell but he, very sensitive and almost dominated by his mother, agreed and left. Every month he sent money home, the house from which he had finally left. His mother only ever called him around the twenty-seventh of the month. Not to ask him how she was, but to demand that the money be sent. All in all, leaving home, breathing different air, meeting new people had regenerated him. What is the point in this story? That the famous emotional tank had not been emptied, it was there ready to explode. Like a bomb from the Second World War, the kind that can still be found today and detonated by the bomb squad. Take this metaphor away, put it in your pocket. It fits wonderfully. After two years of this Edo finds a girl who was there on holiday and came from a town about twenty kilometers away from her. It's love at first sight and after just over a month she decides to give a new twist to her life. He finds work in a hotel near his home and goes to live with Lia. In the meantime, his parents' situation has also improved and he has even resumed relations with his sister. In the years spent in that hotel we said that the emotional tank remained full of negative emotions that were associated in his mind with the actions of everyday working life. In short, he started constantly changing jobs, returning home, albeit in different conditions, was stimulating those emotions again. It wasn't long before she got back together with her family and the conflicts with her mother also resumed. The anxiety had started to rise again, Edoardo began to become intractable even with Lia. He gets nervous every time he gets a call from his mother. So instead of distancing himself from it, he continues to remain in this dynamic of conflict and nervousness. Until he arrives. Panico decides that it's time to change the cards in Edo's life. She starts visiting him at work and he starts to hate that job. He decides to change various jobs, in other sectors but Panico continues to not leave him, just as his mother does not leave him who starts to interfere in her private life as if her son's new life bothers her. Edoardo then decides to go to a therapist who, after a few conversations, understands that the source of stress is her mother. She then invites him to break off relations. At least for a while. The psychologist's request creates many conflicts in the mind of our protagonist. Mom is always mom, you know. Initially, therefore, try in every way to re-establish a peaceful relationship. But Panic is always there, when he visits him he freezes and becomes stiff as a log, as soon as he regains some mobility he also cries like a fountain. Often his encounters with Panico occur following calls or dinners with his parents. So he finally decides that the time has come to cut the umbilical cord. Panic disappears, he has accomplished his mission. Edoardo is well and calm. He is emptying his emotional tank thanks to the therapeutic process, he does not take calming drugs and continues his life peacefully. From time to time, once a year he visits his mother without suffering any reactions.

This case is very similar to Lucia's in the sense that the basic work was the same, the source of discomfort lay in family relationships but unlike Lucia, Edoardo chooses therapy even if it involves taking an almost unnatural step, detaching himself from mother. Why does the psychologist give this address to Edoardo? It's very simple. The therapist identifies the source of discomfort and at the same time understands that he must empty his tank of negative emotions before resuming relationships.

Edoardo would never have done it of his own free will. This makes us understand that everything depends on us and our internal state. There are phases in life when you have to abstain from something and then reintroduce it in small doses. Some understand it, some don't. We arrive at situations where relational conflict becomes a constant and is accepted as normal. When this happens, the emotional tank never runs dry. I could use the metaphor of food intolerances. When I had my gastritis due to stress and Panic's visits, I couldn't drink coffee, eat dairy products or drink alcohol. Or rather, I could choose to do it but then I would pay the consequences. After abstaining from these foods for more than six months I began gradually reintroducing them into my diet, in moderation. They were foods that I liked, so I felt the discomfort of deprivation. But at the same time I knew that the excruciating pain caused by taking them in a given period was far less bearable than the feeling of deprivation. Telling his parents I don't want to see you anymore, don't look for me, don't call me, we're done until further notice wasn't easy for Edoardo, but time fixes things and thanks to that detachment he is now more serene and can rebuild a new type of relationship with the family. We can also call this reconstruction "rewriting history" and it is very important to rewrite the emotions associated with something or someone. When we experience strong

conflict in the birth family, we run the high risk of repeating those situations in the family and in the relationships we are going to create. Ergo. If I witness arguments between my parents for a long time, it is very likely that in my child or adolescent mind the association life as a couple = argument = arguments = separation is created. Unconsciously, therefore, the tendency to attract subjects who vibrate at that frequency develops. The result is the argument between the couple. It's obvious. It seems absurd, the motivation that triggers the reproduction of these behaviors is nostalgia. Nostalgic for what? Of childhood. So much so that many parents make their children do what they would have liked to do as children. It is, allow me to say, a slightly distorted form of the concept of reworking and rewriting emotions. In some cases it's the worst thing that can happen. The parent transfers his childhood dreams to his child. Let's take a trivial but fitting example.
If as a child you really wanted to learn to play the guitar but it wasn't bought for you, you will tend to want to direct your child, almost forcing it on him, to play the guitar. Projection onto someone. It's a constant. The projection of something onto others is given by the lack of work on oneself. From the lack of reworking, you have to rewrite on your own mind not on that of others. Your emotions depend on the type of your thoughts. I will dedicate a chapter to this shortly. I will share with you concepts, attitudes

and research that have helped me in personal growth. I will do it because I think it is important. It is a keystone that will open many doors for you. There are still a couple of testimonies left to tell. One is that of Mario, who experiences encounters with Panico every time he meets a new girl. The other is that of Giada, a girl who was a victim of bullying during her adolescence and encountered Panic every time she met three scoundrels (I don't know how else to define them, although I am aware of having to abstain from judgment as much as possible).

The story of Mario and Panico begins precisely following those tumultuous family relationships between his parents, so we connect a little to the considerations made a few lines ago. Mario is an only child, the classic "mama's boy", he lives a very happy childhood and is also very close to his grandfather. When he becomes a teenager, family harmony changes abruptly. It turns out that the father, an upright and irreproachable man of one piece, is cheating on his mother with another woman. He begins to witness arguments between the parents, the betrayed mother seeks support from the young boy, seeks a shoulder, feels betrayed, feels anger towards her husband who no longer hides. He leaves the house saying that he is going to his lover. Even in front of Mario he feels helpless. When this happens, at least three evenings a week, the mother verbally attacks her father in front of her son, she looks like a lioness, screams, curses and insults. When her father leaves the gate with the car, the woman collapses into long and heartbreaking cries, and often the shoulder on which she cries is Mario's. The story goes on for years and Mario grows up. During those years unconsciously, the reality that is written in his mind regarding relationships is extremely negative. Her mother suffers from her, she becomes depressed, he doesn't know what to do, he sees her taking these drops, losing weight, dragging herself around the house like a ghost. He begins to argue and enter into conflict with his father, who tries to minimize it by inviting him and his mother to accept his extramarital affair by taking it a little philosophically. He feels like a great man, even though his life partner is ill, he doesn't seem to be affected by it, he lives his life like any self-respecting narcissist. But life through other entities has a nice surprise in store for him. One fine day his lover leaves him. She rejects him out of the blue. He tries in every way to continue but there is no chance of victory. The pride of a narcissist burns strongly, at home he is nervous, eats little and in a hurry, often holds his head in his hands and says nothing to his wife and son. But after a couple of weeks of no longer leaving the house, his wife and Mario give up. Why doesn't he go away anymore? Why does he hold his head in his hands like a beaten dog? Do you want to see what's over? This is enough for the mother to say goodbye to depression that in a couple of days she packs her bags and leaves her mind. Ironically where do you think this depression is going? Maybe you've already guessed it...yes exactly, she goes to her husband. He settles in his mind and unpacks the bags that he had packed shortly before in the mind of the poor betrayed wife. Man is now literally a rag, like Icarus without his wax wings. Flat like a punctured tire. The wife is happy, she finds enormous relief in the situation, and she looks after her husband by lending him the drops that she had been using until a few days before because of her. He had betrayed her, he had hurt her, he had ignored her and had been deaf to her requests and yet now she was there, taking care of her man, and mind you that she didn't do it out of mercy, but for the joy of to see him reduced as she had been reduced. A bit of healthy sadism. Taking care of him, pitying him, encouraging him to react, telling him that he should take it philosophically constituted her revenge, which is why we speak in jargon of the "sweet taste of revenge". In all this Mario found a sort of relief, his family was reunited again. Unconsciously, however, the mental associations that he had created had been sculpted in a very incisive way and seeing the father in that state was yet another reinterpretation of the association between relationship = suffering = depression. First the mother, now the father. The focus was there, on depression resulting from an emotional relationship. With these premises you must have already understood what happened to Mario afterwards. By now your knowledge on the topic allows you to understand that the protagonist of this story has an emotional tank full of slime and not having rewritten and reworked in his mind the associations created over the years with regard to relationships, he is practically marked. Destined not to live well in any relationship as a couple. The unconscious fear of reaching the consequences that he has seen with his eyes and felt on his skin creates what they call self-sabotage. When does self-sabotage happen?

We've talked about cellular memory several times, right? We said that if we associate a certain intonation with a key, every time we press that key we always get the same note, ad infinitum. Well.

What emotions did Mario associate with the topic of romantic relationships? Sadness, anger, anxiety, depression, conflicts etc.

As we said, our brain learns and develops largely by creating associations. With experience we learn that if we touch a pot on the stove with boiling water without a glove we get burned. Therefore, if you see the pan on the stove, don't touch it with your bare hands because you know you'll get burned. Paradoxically, if there was a pot on the stove and you were forced to touch it, you would start to feel the pain even before touching it. Because your brain already knows you're going to feel bad. The intent of a threat or blackmail is based precisely on this leverage. We feel bad just at the thought of evil. Right? How do they do it in a criminal interrogation? You've seen it a thousand times on television. There is one tied to a chair and another brandishing something sharp or capable of offending, under the threat of pain information is obtained. Well.

But what does this have to do with self-sabotage? Everything, it's all here. To avoid something associated with pain, the brain tries to distance you from it. This happens when a normal version of experiences is not rewritten onto it. Do you understand now how important it is to rework? Do you realize why if you don't have this knowledge you have to go to therapy?

Mario is one of those who occasionally goes to a psychologist, has a couple of meetings and then disappears. Panic for him is always constantly lurking. He hasn't been able to get it out yet. But he is patient, he waits for us where he knows that sooner or later we will return. In the case of emotional relationships, someone chooses not to experience them anymore. Problem solved. Panic awaits you there and you step out of the way. You solved the panic attacks. But you know you won't be able to afford that thing anymore. You don't deserve it. If you're okay with that, amen, you're in charge. It's all here. It's a shame, however, that love in life is not just a need, an essential nourishment, it is also a right. You have the right to love. Pets, volunteer activities, Toyland, are all anesthetizing. However, know that if in the book of your life it is written that you have to do that specific thing or experience there are no Saints or Madonnas as they say. Mario reaches states of emotional tension that almost lead to exhaustion in certain cases. Then when the story doesn't take off he complains. After years of trying, it happens that he just can't handle a romantic relationship. He approaches, writes, messages, goes out and after these phases the frustration begins. His internal saboteur just doesn't let him start the actual relationship. There is never a first time. It's as if in the previous metaphor women were the pot on the fire, he would like to touch her but his brain blocks him. It seems like he's telling him: - "stop, you'll get burned, don't touch her, she'll burn, the relationship is anxiety, sadness, anger, arguments, depression... it's not for you" - or rather - "it's not for me" - so after a few meetings in which he would always like to go further, Panic arrives and paralyzes him. He goes to the doctor, gets a prescription for drops and ends the relationship. Then he goes out again and tells everyone that he is fine, that he is happy now. But it's not true, he doesn't accept having to be alone. But in order to no longer be alone, Panico demands reworking, Panico knows that he must change the associations in his mind or he won't move forward. He is waiting for you at the gate. Can you live like this? If you want, yes, but watch out for time... it passes and doesn't stop for an hour. Time moves forward. Tick tock tick tock. Do you feel anguish? Open the lock on the cage and exit. The key is in your pocket, check carefully. Only you can take it and open it. Not even this book can save you. What do you want to do?

Mario decided to stay there again. It's a choice, his choice. And everyone in his life does what he wants, just avoid complaining though. Every time he meets me he asks me for advice, and I always give him the same. He would like you to indulge him, to agree with him. But I'm not so. I tell you my truth. This is therefore the testimony of an unsolved case, of an appointment postponed until the next one or never again with Panico. This is also a possibility as mentioned. I want to give you the tools to go and look for him as I already told you, I want to give you the racket to play matches with him. But you're the one playing. It is you who has to use the racket, it is you who goes to the playing field, you know where or who Panic resides in your life. It can be easy to avoid if he is tied to a place, you no longer go to that place and you no longer have Panic visits. However, pay attention to what you have written in your mind in that place, pay attention to the associations that have been created and above all pay attention to your emotional tank. In these testimonies we have linked Panic to work, to the profession. Not necessarily stressed professions, but places where you simply spend a lot of your time and where you go with all your inner baggage. Panic attacks occur in adulthood. From twenty years old and up. So it doesn't depend on the job regardless. However, if that workplace is the place from which you escape so as not to encounter Panic, then before entering another workplace, make sure you empty your tank of negative emotions and make sure you understand that the bond connected to the place remains in that place. place, otherwise you risk carrying it with you all the time. If you then take it with you wherever you go then you can't escape, because it doesn't escape from you. So analyze this aspect too. Now let's see the story of Giada and her encounter with Panico linked to those three "good girls" who tormented her. When she was in middle school, Giada was going through a moment of family discomfort due to the separation between her parents. This often generates discomfort in children due to an unmotivated sense of guilt that seems to arise unconsciously in children. The reaction that follows in many cases leads to the onset of discomfort in the form of requests for attention. Some children, traumatized by the events, hope in their purity and innocence that their parents can thus be reunited. However, this is not enough to recall what was once defined as a "sense of responsibility". Unfortunately, many do not have it. Even for these ways of being I will continue to abstain from judgments and considerations. Being a parent is an experience that I don't have so I don't talk about it, I only talk about what I know. Our Giada was therefore the classic introverted child at school, always a little sad who kept to herself. This passive attitude of hers made her a victim of bullying by three of her peers who were in the same school as her. The bully is not as strong an individual as one might think, he is usually a loser who targets weak and isolated individuals. To face them you just need to react decisively and attack them head-on, this discourages them from getting closer. If, however, they find easy prey, who doesn't react, the sense of strength in them, who are not strong, grows out of all proportion. Every time they commit an abuse they feed their need for strength. In many cases they suffer from an inferiority complex. Usually they surround themselves with at least one accomplice until they form real packs. These packs almost never clash with another pack. They almost always target single individuals or groups of fewer people. I gloss over the behavior that I consider inappropriate of teachers and society in general with regard to this. The way that is used to address the topic only worsens the various situations, to the point of even fueling them. This, however, is another topic. Let's go back to Giada. Having understood that she did not react, and seeing that the teachers did not intervene to resolve the problem, every day they targeted her with teasing, pulling and various humiliations. For Giada it went from bad to worse. Every morning it was a drama to take her to school. She was terrified of the idea of coming into contact with her tormentors, plus she continued to suffer from her parents' separation. Soon Panico arrived to save her. Since the adults were unable to face and block the problem, he took care of saving her. She had spoken to her parents several times about the drama she was experiencing. In an initial phase, both her mother and father had attempted to minimize her problem by inviting her to present these requests to the teachers. Which she had done, but the teachers, almost annoyed by her requests for help, had identified her as a nuisance, and as a recreation they made her stay close to them, isolating her from the others. This 'brilliant' solution only made things worse. The three used the situation to harass her even more precisely because she spent recess escorted, so to speak, by adults. In the time of internet chats and everything elsc, the torment didn't end with the return home and Giada was getting worse and worse. So the parents finally decided to talk to the principal. But nothing happened, she claimed to know about the problem but at the same time that she couldn't do anything. She limited herself to summoning the parents of the three to invite them to speak with their daughters, but according to the old adage 'like father, like son'. Her parents took it badly, as if the victims were her daughters and threatened to sue her, adding insult to injury to her. Fortunately, Panico's interventions became more and more insistent and acute, he was his only ally. The only escape route. The janitors, not the teachers, started calling the ambulance every time the little girl froze and she couldn't breathe. The arrival of the ambulance several times later forced the parents to sort things out, transferring the little girl to another institution. I say. Did she want it that much? Thanks to Panico, the arrival of the ambulance forced them to leave work in shifts and go to hospital. At that point and only at that point did they decide to dedicate the right amount of time to their daughter and resolve the issue. Alleluia.

Needless to say, Panico had resolved the issue this time too. The little girl's displeasure for her parents remained there and as she grew up Giada managed to process and get over the suffering, but Panico no longer visited her in the new school, on the contrary, she found a small group of friends with whom she could talk and discuss and feel good . End of the story.

Also in this testimony we saw how Panic was not the problem but the solution to address the issue and save the situation.

This is why I define us who are or have been "the Panic", of the "Elect".

Panic gives us the chance to understand that something is wrong and the time has come to stop suffering and change things. He forces you by force. And you know it well. But maybe it's the only way he has to get our attention. The techniques that I have shared with you are used to learn to dialogue with him when he comes in front of you and you are "Face to face with Mr. Panic's attacks" as the title of this very modest work of mine states. The rest of the book helps you change your perspective, or rather completely overturn it. You can use it as a mantra, "Panic is not the problem, it's the solution!"

At this point my darling, I would write the final word.

If my techniques and everything else I have told you will help you, I am sure that you will be able to help others after you have helped yourself thanks to Mr. Panic.

Good work.

A hug, Romolo Persichetti.

A special thank you for the collaboration goes to my sponsor Pax Lux Design & Fashion which you can find on Ebay.

Index:

Preface

 1. Chapter 1: How I consider Panic and how I met it
 2. Chapter 2 : Lowering your guard

www.ingramcontent.com/pod-product-compliance
Lightning Source LLC
Chambersburg PA
CBHW070806260726
48660CB00005B/1730